THE MADWOMAN OF BERESINA

Borgo Press Books by FRANK J. MORLOCK

The Chevalier d'Éon and Other Short Farces from the Eighteenth- and Nineteenth-Century French Theatre (Editor)
Chuzzlewit
Congreve's Comedy of Manners
Crime and Punishment
Cyrano and Molière: Five Plays by or About Molière (Editor)
Falstaff (with William Shakespeare, John Dennis, and William Kendrick)
Fathers and Sons
The Idiot
Jurgen
Justine
Lord Jim
The Madwoman of Beresina and Other Napoleonic Plays (Editor)
Notes from the Underground
Oblomov
Old Creole Days
Outrageous Women: Lady Macbeth and Other French Plays (Editor)
Peter and Alexis
The Princess Casamassima
A Raw Youth
The Stendhal Hamlet Scenarios and Other Shakespearean Shorts from the French (Editor)
Two Voltairean Plays: The Triumvirate and Comedy at Ferney (Editor)
The Widow's Husband; and, Porthos in Search of an Outfit: Two Dumasian Comedies (Editor)

THE MADWOMAN OF BERESINA

AND OTHER NAPOLEONIC PLAYS

FRANK J. MORLOCK, EDITOR

THE BORGO PRESS
MMXIII

THE MADWOMAN OF BERESINA

Copyright © 2000, 2007, 2012, 2013 by Frank J. Morlock

FIRST EDITION

Published by Wildside Press LLC

www.wildsidebooks.com

DEDICATION

For my friend and doctor, Al Segal

CONTENTS

THE MADWOMAN OF BERESINA, by
    Emmanuel Théaulon and Honoré de Balzac . . . 9
CAST OF CHARACTERS. 10
ACT I. 11
ACT II 55
THE END OF MURAT, by Jean Berleux and
    Alexandre Dumas. 85
CAST OF CHARACTERS. 86
AUTHOR'S PREFACE. 88
SCENE I 89
SCENE II. 101
SCENE III 127
THE TRIAL OF MARSHAL NEY, by Louis-
    Marie Fontan and Charles Dupeuty 133
CAST OF CHARACTERS. 134
SCENE I 136
SCENE II. 155

SCENE III 166
SCENE IV 179
ABOUT THE EDITOR 187

THE MADWOMAN OF BERESINA

BY EMMANUEL THÉAULON
AND HONORÉ DE BALZAC

CAST OF CHARACTERS

COLONEL FALBERT

THE SURGEON-IN-CHIEF of the Army

BARON, brother-in-law of the Countess

VALET de Chambre

COUNTESS DE VANDIÈRES

ROSINE, her femme de chambre

A PAGE

Female Guests, Army Officers, Valets, Soldiers

ACT I

An expensive salon with a portrait of Czar Alexander I over the chimney at the back. Two windows opening on the Kremlin. Side doors, armchairs, etc.

AT RISE, Rosine and Fleuriot are looking through the windows at the rear. Military music is heard.

FLEURIOT

To Moscow! We are in Moscow and the Emperor is passing in review on the Kremlin Square—the Carrousel of this country.

ROSINE

And after the review the Countess de Vandières, my mistress, is giving a ball at the major estate of the Emperor.

FLEURIOT

In the salons of the Kremlin where we are lodged! A military party day and night—of which I am the organizer in chief, in my capacity as secretary to the Countess. A French ball in Moscow. That could be seen only under the reign of the Emperor. Long live the Emperor! That's my man. They say he's going to do a world tour at double time. I'm not against it!

ROSINE

Here comes Doctor Fournier, Surgeon-General to the Grand Army. He's with Colonel Falbert, you know!

FLEURIOT

Yes, yes, I know.

ROSINE

I'm going to inform the Countess and prepare her dress for the ball.

FLEURIOT

I'm not against that. (Rosine leaves.) (To Colonel Falbert and the Surgeon-General who enter) Well! Colonel! They insisted we'd never reach Moscow! Here we are already, and I was one of the first thirty thousand men to enter.

COLONEL

Yes, Mr. Fleuriot, we are in Moscow, in the sacred palace of the Czars.

SURGEON-GENERAL

Is the Countess visible, Mr. Fleuriot?

FLEURIOT

I don't think she's returned, sir.

COLONEL

What! At the moment of giving a ball!

FLEURIOT

Is she ever in one place? She's a real sylphide. You think she's in her boudoir, she's at a parade. You imagine she's in Paris, she's cruising through the streets of Moscow. And the moment she ought to be present to receive the persons she's invited to her military ball, she's nowhere to be found. I bet she went to the ambulances to provide care to the wounded. Just yesterday she obtained bounties from His Majesty, mercy for three Russian wretches they were going to shoot. In the end she's an angel disguised as a woman.

SURGEON-GENERAL

To whom are you speaking?

FLEURIOT (maliciously)

It's not to you I'm speaking to—it's to Colonel-Count

Falbert.

SURGEON-GENERAL

Fleuriot.

FLEURIOT

No one is unaware that the Colonel grew up with the Countess at Vandières, and that he ought to have married her; but our Emperor, who has eyes everywhere, who sees all, hears all, discovers your fiancée in a château in the Pyrenees where she was living with an old aunt; and, as she had a great name, he wanted to marry her to one of his great men, the brave general, the Count de Vandières.

COLONEL

Oh! Brave like his sword.

FLEURIOT

Agreed. And they say the Emperor is going to give him a Marshal's baton. I'm not opposed to it. But to make him marry at his age—'cause he's old like French glory—a young girl of seventeen—

COLONEL

Enough, enough, Fleuriot. You are reviving all my sorrows. Yes, doctor, separated from Julie who I loved more than life, I threw myself into the career of arms. I followed our victorious armies everywhere. I sought death in every battle.

FLEURIOT

And there you found the epaulettes of a Colonel, and the title of First Orderly to the Emperor. I much prefer that for you.

SURGEON-GENERAL

The young countess gave you the example of courage; with what noble devotion she consecrated herself to the old general; she wanted to follow him in all his campaigns. Share his dangers, ease him in his weariness, in his sufferings; and the Emperor who knows the fine character of Madame de Vandières has done nothing to prevent it. On the contrary, he's used her himself on several occasions, and more than once by his order, the sound of joyous instruments have followed, as today, the roar of cannons.

COLONEL (confidentially to the doctor)

I've come to bring her news of the general, and perhaps, this time, Julie will be less severe to the friend of her childhood. Would you believe, doctor, that this woman, so weak in appearance, who resembles a child, displays such character, such firmness, that I, a man, a soldier, don't have myself. For nearly three months since I found her in the train of our army, she's avoided me with a care that makes me despair; she treats me with an indifference that I have trouble conceiving, and yet, I admit to you, I flattered myself that she shared the sorrow that her marriage plunged me into.

FLEURIOT

(at the back) I perceive that the Countess is in the salons; she's examining the preparations for the ball.

COLONEL (looking)

Who's that she's talking with?

SURGEON-GENERAL

You don't recognize him? The brother of the Count de Vandières, the Inspector General of Posts of the Army.

FLEURIOT

The most sensitive man to cold in the Empire, about whom it is said—as for me, I think he's a coward who blames his trembling on the cold. We have many administrators with that sort of strength.

(sings)

In these climes we look about us

And see our unfortunate fighters trembling with—

cold.

But the fire of roaring cannons

Is coming to warm our infantry and cavalry

So they'll still think they're in their foyers

Under the ramparts of an immense fire

Braving winter and its rigors.

It's the moment when the firing recommences

That we see our brave contractors shiver.

COLONEL

Here's Julie!

JULIE (entering)

Come on, that's very nice. Our ball will be charming. Hello, doctor. (noticing the Colonel) Ah, Colonel, it's you. (a mixture of fear and pleasure can be seen on her face) I thought you were on a mission. (aside) Poor Falbert! What a sad and unhappy look he has!

BARON (shivering and going to the chimney)

Gentlemen, I am indeed honored to greet you. Brr! It's cold, it's cold.

COLONEL (who's gone close to Julie)

Last night I received the order to return to Headquarters, and I must congratulate myself on it, because I'll be able to see you shine (slightly ironic) in this new fest.

JULIE (heavily)

This fest! The Emperor wanted it, and I am the most submissive of his lieutenants, because in like circumstances, it's always he who calls you like this. Judge what an honor it is for me— Are you bringing me news of the general?

COLONEL

I left him at the outposts between Kervo and Gradne— three hours distance from Moscow.

BARON

Already on the road to Saint Petersburg. Brr! I'm shivering just at the thought of it.

SURGEON-GENERAL

In that case Baron, don't think of it. Besides, we have all winter to think of it, because the old capital of the Czars is indeed ours, after so many troubles, after so many struggles.

JULIE

Oh! I'll never forget the enthusiasm with which the army was carried away when, from the heights of Mont-Salut, which dominates Moscow, they perceived this great city, half-oriental, half-European, with its eight hundred churches, with its thousand clocks, its golden cupolas that sparkle in the Sun. At this appearance, our soldiers, struck with astonishment and admiration, as before their companions before Thebes of the Hundred Gates, shouted, clapping their hands, "Moscow! Moscow!" Thirty thousand men entered the city singing, "The Day of Glory has come."

COLONEL

The next day the army had forgotten all its labors, but the city is rich, well-provisioned, and we've found five hundred empty palaces, with their servants having orders to serve us as their masters. Our stay here resembles a story in the Arabian Nights. And the illusion is completed by seeing you, Madame, for you are the fairy of the Army of which the Emperor is the Genie.

FLEURIOT (aside)

Hang yourself, Fleuriot, you haven't found that one.

JULIE (generously)

You are a flatterer, Colonel Falbert. And the Emperor

performs prodigies—whereas I— Did General Vandières seem to you to be satisfied with the position of his Army Corps?

COLONEL

You know that the general is not very communicative on all matters concerning these great questions. He spoke to me only of you, Madame. And several times expressed regret to me that he felt for having brought you to Moscow. It's for you he fears weariness, the rigor of the climate, the perils of the war.

BARON (as before)

Brr! It's cold, it's cold!

JULIE

I hope you reassured him, Colonel. I haven't yet noticed the change in climate. As for the rest—

(singing)

What do I care about peril?

What do I care about suffering?

My happiness is to follow

An admired spouse.

And to see the standards of our beautiful France

Surrounded everywhere with glory and respect.

A daughter of a soldier,

Wife of a general.

I still love war

The way I love a ball.

In our wars in Spain,

I danced the bolero, the fandango.

In our German conquests

I danced, I danced

The Allemande, and waltzed.

In London, it will be the English.

In the end, by serving the Emperor

Before long I will know

All the dances of the earth!

Ah! What glory, what joy!

Daughter of a soldier,

Wife of a General.

I love war

Like I love a ball.

As for me, in the same victory

I love to join the palms of glory,

With the roses of pleasure.

So long as the cannons roar I'm here, I'm here!

The violin replies I am there! I am there!

Dance and please.

Ah, that's charming.

After war,

A ball is ravishing.

SURGEON-GENERAL (to Fleuriot)

What a charming little lady!

FLEURIOT (low)

And to say this fellow was given seniority of rank.

JULIE (to doctor)

You will be of our party, doctor?

SURGEON-GENERAL

Impossible, Countess, my duty claims me. The Russians, in leaving Moscow, left thirty thousand of their wounded in my hands.

FLEURIOT

And our grenadiers wound well.

SURGEON-GENERAL

To whom are you saying that?

VALET (enters, announcing)

A Page from the Emperor.

(Valet leaves, Page enters)

PAGE

His Majesty is calling for the Inspector General of Army Posts.

COLONEL (aside)

Great: he will leave me alone with Julie.

BARON

I am presenting myself to his august person. (aside) The Devil take him. This Colonel is going to be alone with my sister.

PAGE

His Majesty is also calling for Colonel Falbert.

BARON (aside)

Good!

COLONEL (aside)

I shall spy out the favorable moment. (aloud) Come on,

Gentlemen. (sings)

When the Emperor's voice calls us,

We must swiftly give in to his desire,

To prove to him our respect and zeal.

By not hesitating to leave pleasures.

JULIE (singing)

Don't forget, gentlemen, that our fest

Must have a mad success.

What can be greater in these days of conquest

Than the French dancing in Moscow?

ALL

When the Emperor calls, etc.

(all leave except Julie, who collapses onto a divan.)

JULIE

Falbert! He will be at this fest! I was hoping not to see him again in the absence of my husband. And in the trouble I am in, in the sadness that carries me away, so long as I no longer have anyone with whom to show off my feigned gaiety? When he's far from me, I get down. I resume my courage and once again I become the companion of a hero. So long as the Colonel reappears, I'll become a child again and I no longer have anything but tears.

(she weeps)

ROSINE

You are weeping again, my good mistress.

JULIE (rising and trying to dry her tears.)

I cannot hide my pain from you, Rosine; your friendship is so touching and so devoted. You, the companion of my childhood, who left everything to follow me. Yes, I was weeping because I was alone—and I saw him again! You know that in his presence and despite all my efforts I no longer have courage.

ROSINE

You must have it, Madame, for perhaps courage was never more necessary.

JULIE

What do you mean?

ROSINE

Frightful rumors are circulating on all sides. They are saying that the Emperor allowed himself to be led into a trap. That the Russian army is enveloping us on all sides, and that we'll never see France again.

JULIE

Who has actually been able to employ such language, Rosine? At the very moment when everything seems to favor us, the day in which our arms are triumphant everywhere, and when the Emperor is so great, so formidable. Oh, no, no—the star that guides him is not ready to go pale. And yet, I must tell you, Rosine, these rumors are in accord with frightful omens, and if I believed in dreams— Oh! But I don't believe it, Rosine; I don't want to believe it.

ROSINE

The Emperor himself believes it, and as for me, I believe it, too. If Miss Lenormand were here, she could tell you— What was it you actually dreamed, Madame?

JULIE

Listen, and don't laugh at my weakness. You recall that in coming to Moscow we crossed a river covered with ice floes?—and no one was able to tell us what its name was?

ROSINE

I remember that.

JULIE

Well, last night in a dream, I saw the same river again.

ROSINE

Ah!

JULIE

Listen.

(sings)

I dreamed of this terrible river

And its waves, growling and troubled

Dragging down, O horrible sight!

Our bloody, mutilated soldiers.

Trembling, I asked

"What is this river?"

Beside me, a shivering voice screamed

"It's the Beresina,

It's the Beresina."

And the echo twice repeated

"It's the Beresina,

It's the Beresina."

ROSINE

The Beresina.

JULIE

Oh, Rosine, that's not all.

(sings)

The frightful laughter of the demented

Now escaped from my breast.

With great screams I called France.

I called again, but in vain.

Delirium exploded

In my burning head.

Then I began to sing and dance

Saying "There she is—

It's the Beresina,

It's the Beresina."

And France, in mourning replies,

"It's the Beresina

It's the Beresina."

ROSINE

Ah, Madame, that dream is frightful. But luckily it's only a dream.

JULIE

Yes, yes, you are right. It's only a dream.

(music)

Come on, Rosine, now's the time

We are becoming the Countess de

Vandières again. My hair is pretty,

Isn't it? With grenades. Our good

Grenadiers will love it?

(aside)

It's the flower that he prefers.

(aloud)

Rosine—my gloves, my bouquet.

(Rosine gives them to her)

Oh, how pretty it is, Rosine. They were picked in the magnificent greenhouses of the Kremlin.

And it's the Emperor who deigned to send them to me by means of his favorite page. But for him, it would have been the first time I appeared at a ball without a bouquet. Because in Moscow—

ROSINE

The Emperor thinks of everything, Madame. And they say that this morning he signed a decree regarding the Comédie Française.

JULIE

Are they going to be proud, the actors—to see themselves the object of a decree dated Moscow.

(Drum beats)

What's that?

FLEURIOT (entering)

The review is over and the Emperor is reentering the Kremlin.

BARON (rushing in)

Sis, I am coming in all haste to warn you that his Majesty is going to appear at your ball; his face is all radiant.

JULIE (soulfully)

Oh—so much the better!

FLEURIOT

Business isn't going too badly, as they say down there.

BARON

Our position is superb, my dear; we shall spend the winter peacefully in Moscow, at the fireside, and in the Spring we'll go to India and drive out the English.

FLEURIOT

I'm not opposed to that.

VOICES (off)

Long live The Emperor!

(Music for the Chorus begins)

JULIE

The Emperor! Let's hurry to the ballroom.

(Julie leaves)

FLEURIOT

As for me, I'm returning to my duties as director of the Fest. (he leaves)

(At the back, The Emperor and his aides pass by, but

are only visible through the glass.)

CHORUS (off)

Behold the son of victory,

The hope, the love, the honor of France!

To our France he gave Glory,

While waiting to give it peace.

BARON (alone)

Yes, he's a great man! But he ought not to meddle in our family affairs. Let him conquer Russia, India, and the whole world, if he chooses; I shall say like Fleuriot, "I'm not opposed to that...." But what need had he to marry my illustrious brother at his age? This young Colonel worries me. He loved my sister-in-law before her marriage, and it's not impossible that he was loved. Whatever may be, I must watch over the honor of my illustrious brother, and since he cannot be here, I'll be here. Two hundred thousand francs income, that's such a fine dowry. My brother made a fortune more rapidly than I did, and yet, in something close, our careers are the same. He's the general of a division; I'm Inspector General of Army Posts. There's a general on both sides.

(sings)

Yes, the two of us, in many a big deal.

You can see us climbing with the same passion.

Because both of us greatly love war.

Proud of marching on the path of honor.

With an equal zeal to reach glory,

We lead French battalions.

As for him, he said, "Let's march to victory"

Meanwhile, I prepared the relays.

JULIE (entering, aside)

What mystery. I'm still upset over it. In the confusion of the ball, a stranger just delivered to me this letter in secret. What can they want of me?

(about to open it)

Heavens—the Baron—Let's move him away.

(aloud)

Aren't you going to dance, Baron?

BARON (with asperity)

My dear sister knows very well that I never dance.

JULIE

Oh, that's annoying. Because the Emperor has expressed to me several times the desire to see you dance. And just now, again.

BARON

Truly? He's too busy, that great man. I will dance, sis, I will dance, since that may please him. It's possible he has some great idea involving me that seizes him like that. I will dance. (he dances by himself to music off stage). I'm going to dance immediately to prove to him my respect. (leaves dancing)

JULIE

(alone, rapidly opening the letter) Let's read: "You are my good angel. I owe you my life and I find myself lucky in the ability to meet such a great benefit through the warning I am going to give you. Hasten to make yourself ready to depart and leave Moscow when you can without danger. Tomorrow at dawn it will be too late—the French Army will, perhaps, no longer exist." Great God! This advice—who can be giving it to me? One of those wretched Russians for whom I've obtained mercy? No doubt.

But perhaps they want to terrify me. The Emperor is calm, and yet what interest could this foreigner have? This mysterious letter must be shown to the Emperor.

But to him alone. If this frightful news were to spread.... Yes, it must be a mystery to the whole world—even from the Colonel.

(the music stops)

It's him!

COLONEL (entering, aside, joyfully)

She's alone.

JULIE (aside)

Let's get back to the ball?

COLONEL

You are avoiding me, Julie.

JULIE

I'm afraid my absence may be noticed.

COLONEL

Do you refuse to receive my goodbyes, my last goodbyes, perhaps?

JULIE

You are leaving?

COLONEL

At daybreak.

JULIE

And you barely got here.

COLONEL (with emotion)

Yes, Julie. I'm going to take an order to Marshal Ney, an order to return in all haste to Moscow with the Army Corps he commands.

JULIE

Are we threatened then?

COLONEL

I don't think so. And yet through the calm the Emperor affects, I thought I noticed in him I don't know what unease—

JULIE (aside)

My premonitions are awakened again and that letter—

COLONEL

I am going to leave, and for the first time, I admit to you, I am experiencing, in the performance of my perilous duties, a depression that I cannot define. They say that hordes of Tartars occupy the space that separate us from Marshal Ney, the bravest of the brave. But heaven's my witness that it's not the dangers I'm about to run which cause me unease. Julie—if I go, never to see you again.

JULIE

Falbert!

COLONEL

You are the wife of another man; you create the glory and happiness of a hero that I admire. And since your marriage, Julie, the profession of arms has always seemed to me to be without danger. What does life matter to one who can no longer believe in happiness? And yes, since the fate of battle has reunited us on foreign soil where I see you surrounded by praise and admiration, it seems to me that to stop seeing you would be a greater misfortune for me than that of having lost you.

JULIE

In that case, Falbert, my friend, overcome a weakness that is unworthy of you or of me. We have accepted with resignation the fate that The Emperor's will has assigned us. Why return to the past? Imitate me. I am only a weak woman, and yet I've known how to find courage in my duties to forget the plans we'd made. I am going to make a success of the position of my husband. I've never regarded his age, I've seen only his noble deeds, and the honor of bearing such a glorious name. Yes, I am proud I glory in the choice the Emperor made for me.

COLONEL

No, Julie, no—you never loved me.

JULIE

Ingrate! Is this the language you use with me, you, who since my earliest childhood filled my life at all moments with your image? I never loved you! Ah, in that case, you never understood my heart, never penetrated my thoughts; you've never seen that there was a single thing over my heart—the honor of my spouse. Oh! If I could tell you all that I've suffered; if I could initiate you in my torments, that revive every day now, if I could—but, what's the use of talking! You wouldn't understand my tears because you haven't understood my courage.

(sings)

Every day for the last three years,

Adorned with dazzling flowers,

I seem to be walking,

Surrounded by games, laughter, and love.

And I am queen of every court.

Watching me, watch the flame,

Respect greatness, fortune and honor.

Each can believe in my happiness.

But as for me, I know that my soul

Is full of weariness and sorrow!

(Baron appears at the glass window, observing them.)

COLONEL

Each of your words increases my regret and my admiration for you. Ah, calm down, Julie, henceforth Colonel Falbert will show himself worthy of such tender affection, of such high esteem. Yes, yes, I will keep my sorrow, but from this day forth, I will imitate your courage, and (he kisses her hand)

FLEURIOT (entering and seeing the Baron)

I'm not opposed to it!

(aloud)

Pardon, Madame Countess, but while you are here, the

ball is languishing.

(low)

And your usual spy has his eye on you.

JULIE (aside)

Heavens!

(aloud) Indeed, I was forgetting myself and I thank you for having come to bring me back to myself. Colonel, give me your hand to return to the ball.

BARON (entering)

His Majesty is asking for Colonel Falbert.

COLONEL (aside)

Again! You might say the Emperor is watching over her.

BARON (aside)

They are no longer alone; but I actually saw.—Brr!

JULIE

The Emperor! What new reason?

BARON

It seems that the order is urgent because His Majesty has dispatched three of his pages to find you.

COLONEL

I'll go to him.

JULIE (low, rapidly)

Make him read this note.

COLONEL

This note?

JULIE (low)

Silence! We're being watched,

BARON (aside)

She slipped a love letter to the Colonel.

JULIE

Go take orders from the great man, Colonel. As for me, I'm going back to the ball, more gay, more happy than ever.

(sings)

Pleasure and folly

Be in turn

The order of the day

For my whole life.

((The Colonel leaves with Fleuriot; Julie heads for the ballroom, but is stopped by the Baron)

BARON

One word, as a favor, sis.

JULIE (graciously, laughing)

If it's for a dance, I'm booked up.

BARON

Why, no, no. It's not for a dance. (aside) Let's try to scare her, at least.

JULIE

Come, we can chat during the ball.

BARON

I've only got something brief to tell you.

JULIE

Well, speak, but make it quick, 'cause they're waiting for me.

BARON

The interest that you inspire in me, and the friendship I bear for my illustrious brother makes it my duty to enlighten you about—whimsicality.

(Gesture by Julie)

I'm not speaking of your conduct but your character. I would really like to believe that the respect Colonel Falbert has for you equals the respect that you have for Count de Vandières, and yet appearances—

JULIE (cutting in)

Appearances, sir!

BARON

He's always with you; you affect a noticeable preference for him.

JULIE

No one here is unaware that he was my childhood friend—the general himself—

BARON

Agreed. But in your position, friendship must have limits.

JULIE

Sir, I don't think I've ever forgotten—

BARON

Oh, no. And yet—I can only hope.

JULIE

Explain yourself, Baron, I beg you.

BARON

In the end you wrote in secret to the Colonel.

JULIE

To the Colonel? Me? Ah, yes, yes, just now you saw me give him a letter.

BARON

I saw it by chance, because I beg you to believe—

JULIE

So, sir, it's been well proved to me that you are the

spy in residence over my conduct, surveyor of all my activities. It's horrible, do you know, sir! And if I complained to my husband—

BARON

But, if I too, told him what I saw—

JULIE

Do so, sir, do. Tell the Count that you saw me deliver a note in secret to Colonel Falbert; and if the general honors me with confidence without limit, and wants to know the contents of that letter, the Emperor alone can tell him, because the letter was for him. As for you, Baron, I declare to you that I am revolted by your conduct, and I am releasing you of the need to accompany me—I shall take care of myself very well.

(she goes to the ballroom)

FLEURIOT (coming in with a checkerboard)

Baron—a game of chess?

BARON (aside)

The Devil with it! Crazy woman. Oh, why I won't allow myself to be dazzled by her fine talk.

FLEURIOT

There she is already in her place for the Quadrille—with whom is she dancing there? Heavens, it's with the King of Naples.

BARON

Indeed, it's with Murat—a seducer if there ever was one.

FLEURIOT

Is the old baron afraid his brother will have heirs?

BARON

How cavalierly he leads her, the King of Naples. He is never awkward.—Brr!

FLEURIOT (sings)

What a brilliant ball! What dancers! What glory!

Davoust, Eugene and the brave Essling!

D'Erlon, Murat, the child of victory.

Are together at a ball in the Kremlin.

What great names for a quadrille.

But this pleasure must be allowed them.

Dance, dance, defenders of France,

Yesterday, it was the enemy's turn.

BARON

Well, look here, Mr. Fleuriot, are we going to begin this game of chess?

FLEURIOT

I'm not opposed to it, (goes to table)

(Cannon fire.)

BARON

Brr! now what's that?

(A second shot.)

FLEURIOT

Are the Russians beginning our chess game?

(A third shot.)

JULIE (rushing in)

I wasn't mistaken. Cannons!

BARON (shivering greatly)

By Jove, indeed it is cannon fire.

Brr! Devilish climate, go!

(Cannons)

JULIE (to Baron)

There, there, the reply to the letter you saw me give to the Colonel.

BARON

Believe, truly, Madame that—BRR!

(Cannons continue to be heard until the end of the act.)

PAGE

(enters running followed by ladies) Mr. Inspector of Posts! Horses! Horses for His Majesty and his household. (the ladies of the ball enter and remain at the rear)

The retreat has been decided on, Madame!

(gestures by all)

The Emperor is going on ahead to protect it!

ALL

Great God!

PAGE

Hurry, Mr. Inspector General.

BARON

Right away, sir, right away! (aside) Horses! I'll begin by taking one for myself. Brr!

(he leaves)

FLEURIOT

Now there's a change of face! (buttoning his coat. The call to quarters is heard beating.) My goodness! It seems things are heating up.

(The Surgeon-General enters)

JULIE

(running to him) Ah, it's you, doctor. My husband, sir, my husband?

SURGEON-GENERAL

If I were speaking to an ordinary woman, Madame, I might disguise the truth from her, but towards you I have other duties to fulfill.

JULIE

Ah! What have you come to inform me of?

SURGEON-GENERAL

General Vandières is grievously wounded.

JULIE (with a piercing scream)

Heavens! Where is he, sir, where is he?

SURGEON-GENERAL

I was going to have him brought to your quarters, Madame, when I learned the Emperor had given the signal for the Retreat. I had the general escorted on the road to Smolensk, and I came to inform you.

(Rosine brings Julie her traveling clothes and dresses her, puts a riding cap on her head. Music until the end. Murmuring. The tocsin, the call to arms, cannon fire.)

COLONEL

(entering excitedly, wearing a travel cape) Hurry, or the retreat will be closed to you! Arson is breaking out on all sides. In a few hours Moscow will no longer exist. All the elements seem to unchained against us. Don't worry, Madame Countess, I've been ordered by the Emperor to watch over you, to protect you while the Emperor rushes to stop the Russians at Kalonga.

JULIE (with spirit)

Falbert, Falbert! Save the general, my husband.

COLONEL

I will watch over him and over yourself. I am going to give orders for the departure.

(General confusion and disorder.)

CHORUS OF WOMEN

Save our lives, see our tears.

Protect us in this frightful reversal.

To increase our alarm

Fire is coming to add its flames to Winter.

CHORUS OF MEN

Dry your tears, calm your alarms.

For we are watching over you in this reversal.

(The men leave passing into the gallery to give orders. Confusion.)

JULIE

Oh! Almighty God, protect the hero!

Who alone here can save our army,

And without reversal in our beloved France,

Deign, my God! To bring back our flags.

CHORUS OF WOMEN

O Almighty God, etc.

JULIE

(distracted, to herself) Already, to completely fire my courage,

I see the banks of the Beresina.

(The men return)

GENERAL CHORUS

Let's leave let's leave; joining the Winter,

Everywhere, already, flames are above our heads.

Adding storms to the tumult!

The Enemy is on our heels!

(The tocsin, the call to quarters, and cannon fire are heard at the back. Everyone flees in disorder. At this moment flames light the stage, and the Emperor is seen on the stage. A shout of "Long live the Emperor!" is heard.)

CURTAIN

ACT II

A military tent opening at the back and sides. It takes up little space. Two seats at the back.

ROSINE (allowing the curtain to fall back where she's been looking.)

She's sleeping and we can chat, Mr. Fleuriot.

FLEURIOT

Gladly, Miss Rosine, because all my preparations have been completed.

ROSINE

My poor mistress. Three years of suffering and madness.

FLEURIOT

Ah, my god, yes! Three years have passed—because we crossed the Beresina on November 12, 1812, and today is the first of December, 1815.

ROSINE

Do you think we will succeed, Mr. Fleuriot?

FLEURIOT

The doctor hopes so— He thinks that by tracing before her eyes the picture of the horrible scene that caused her to lose her reason, it may bring about a favorable crisis. Thus Colonel Falbert has made another Beresina river in his park; two hundred soldiers of our old army have worked all summer, and today the Countess will be submitted to this great experiment. The Colonel whose intendant I've become, has spared nothing to make it succeed. It's true, he's rich enough for that, and his uncle left him a small inheritance of a few millions. So he needs none of his pension.

ROSINE

He left it to the new government?

FLEURIOT

For goodness sake! He distributes it to old comrades-in-arms that events have left without resources. They are the ones who must help us today. As for Cossacks, I recruited them in the neighboring villages. On the subject of Cossacks, haven't they had the infamy to say that during the retreat you were seized by a regiment of Kalmucks?

ROSINE

That's not true! I was left with our baggage, you know, through bad luck at Smolensk. The guards took a route that separated me from my mistress, but I reached Paris without incident.

FLEURIOT

I'm not against it. And yet, if you had been captured there, perhaps you'd have gone mad, too, seeing your mistress in that condition. I was close to her, I was! And since that day, I haven't left her until the moment when her brother-in-law Baron Vandières had her shut up in a madhouse in Paris. That old faker, who no longer shivers these days because it's winter in peacetime, was reluctant to consent when the Director of the madhouse brought the Countess to this Château in Picardy. But the Colonel became so enraged that he swore he would unveil the plots of the old Baron, who's designated the administrator of the Countess's estates, to such a degree that the general's brother decided to himself lead his ward to this Château.

ROSINE

When we arrived yesterday evening with the best Doctor from the madhouse, the trip seems to have done my poor mistress good.

FLEURIOT

Yes, but as usual, she doesn't recognize anyone. It was vain for the Colonel to smile at her, talk to her as in their childhood. She seemed a bit afraid of him! And, as for me, since Beresina, she takes me for Napoleon the Great. I'm not opposed to that, but it's quite improbable.

ROSINE

I'm the only one she recognizes.

FLEURIOT

Indeed, I know why.

(low) You're the only one who has all the secrets of her heart. You, and they say—but silence, here's the Colonel.

COLONEL

Well, what! Rosine, you've left your mistress.

ROSINE

She's there in the wing of the Château that you've hidden with this tent. And, she's resting.

COLONEL

Her condition is unchanged?

ROSINE

Unchanged. Now childish, docile, gay. Now sad, capricious, threatening.

COLONEL

Poor Julie!

ROSINE

She constantly demands to go through the gardens and weeps because she's refused.

COLONEL

Soon, I hope, she'll be refused nothing. The image we are going to retrace for her is almost complete. Luckily, the accidents of the terrain have marvelously seconded us. A river crosses through the park of my château. Trees from the North have been transported here at great expense, Down there, on the horizon, the hamlet of Varrière represents the village of Studzanka from which the Russian artillery thundered at our poor soldiers. And Nature, seconding our efforts, has deployed for us, this year, all the riches of Winter.

FLEURIOT

You call these riches, thanks. Three feet of snow everywhere. A wind to smash your skull, and walls of ice. It's another Russia.

COLONEL

Noble Julie! Heaven's my witness that it's not the desire to belong to you one day that is directing me in my glorious enterprise. If I can bring you to yourself, if I can return you to pleasures, to society, I will think myself the happiest of men.

FLEURIOT (who's raised the curtain at the rear)

Colonel.

COLONEL

What is it, my dear Fleuriot?

FLEURIOT

They've forgotten, at the entrance to the forest, the fire with which the Countess tried to revive the old general.

COLONEL

Indeed! Give orders that it be lit right away.

(Fleuriot leaves) Yes, that fire will complete the picture.

I remember that it was also at this bivouac that most of those Marshals of the Empire who saved the wreckage of the army came to warm themselves up.

(sings)

Noble heroes that respected twenty years

The glorious lead of battles

And who, perhaps, in our bloody discords

Will have horrible funerals,

Heaven owes a dazzling death

To these warriors, the glory of our armies.

But, at least, for these old soldiers

Dying by assassinations,

All parties will have tears for them!

ROSINE

Ah, Colonel, the Countess—

COLONEL

Well?

ROSINE

She's coming this way.

COLONEL

What imprudence. Run!

ROSINE

There's no time. Here she is.

(Julie enters, her hair loose on her shoulders, her clothing torn and disarranged; she stops mid-stage and speaks in a tender voice)

JULIE

Goodbye! Goodbye!

COLONEL

Ever the same words she addressed to me on the banks of the river.

JULIE

Goodbye. (she looks around her, and then to the sky as if to see heaven and then the weather.) Ah, finally.

(sings)

Spring brings

Zephyrs and flowers.

Already colors

Shine in the plain.

Already in the shade

The grass grows green

The birds in the bush

Sing their songs once again.

Heaven, purifying itself

Resumes its splendor

Everything in Nature

Is reborn to joy

And everything here says to me

That, at last, a fine day

Will shine on my life.

Tra—la—la.

(she stops singing and remains pensive)

COLONEL (to Rosine)

Go to her gently.

ROSINE

Madame—

JULIE

Ah, there you are, Rosine! Come play on the green of the park. Do you want to?

ROSINE

You know quite well, Madame, that your aunt has forbidden that.

COLONEL (aside, with joy)

That's the first time that memory has come to her mind.

JULIE

Yes, to marry me off—to a general, who will be a Marshal one day. I shall be Madame La Marechale. But, as for me, I prefer to play with you, Rosine, and then, as for him, you know well that I love Falbert so much. Never to see him again, never to think of him. That idea kills me. And for the last three days, I've wept so much. Look at my eyes. Falbert, you see— he's the friend, the companion of my childhood—my mother said to me, "Julie, this is the one who'll be your husband. Love him well." Oh, I love him so much, Rosine. And if it's necessary to leave him, to forget him, I'll die of it. And yet, if I get married as my aunt wants, to the old general, I'll have a beautiful carriage, I'll go to court, to the ball, to war, to the ball.

(she sadly repeats the refrain from the first act)

Daughter of a soldier

Wife of a general

I sill love war—

The way I love

(stops abruptly)

Goodbye! Goodbye!

(rubbing her face impatiently)

Goodbye? Goodbye to whom)

COLONEL (approaching excitedly)

To Falbert.

JULIE

Falbert! Dead! Dead! Falbert! and the other ones,

too. Dead. Down there, before my eyes. Goodbye! Goodbye!

(she bursts out laughing)

Ha, ha, ha!

(resuming her song)

The Spring brings

Zephyrs and flowers.

ROSINE

A foreigner is coming to the tent with Mr. Fleuriot.

COLONEL

Julie must go back in (going to her he wants to take her hand) Julie—

(she flees)

JULIE (childishly)

I don't want to.

COLONEL

What to do?

ROSINE

Wait. The usual way. (she pulls an orange from her pocket and shows it to Julie)

JULIE (delighted)

Ah!

(She advances towards Rosine, hands joined like a child begging. Rosine backs away gently and leads her back the way she came.)

COLONEL

Alas, she's just a child!

FLEURIOT

This way, Doctor, this way.

COLONEL

Doctor Fournier— It's heaven that's sending him.

DOCTOR

My friend.

COLONEL

I'm seeing you again. It's you who've come to me.

Worthy friend—

This new proof of your affection. Oh, you did well to come, because I am the most wretched of men.

DOCTOR

That's why I'm here. Yes. The confusion in your letter struck me. It alarmed my friendship. And I rushed here in all haste.

(The Colonel takes him by the hand)

I would have come sooner, but you know the difficulty of our position. The rest of us former companions of Napoleon—our least actions are misinterpreted and to get a passport you have to have your motives examined. In the end, here I am.

COLONEL

So then, you approve my plan. And you are coming to second it.

DOCTOR

Before approving it or blaming it, my friend, I need to know all the details of this event. Are you certain that Madame de Vandières' madness has for its source the horrible catastrophe that you intend to recreate before her eyes?

(Fleuriot gives the Doctor a chair; the Colonel takes another. Fleuriot remains standing near the Colonel.)

COLONEL

I'll let you judge that, my friend. You know how we were separated at Smolensk. You were called to provide care to numerous wounded in the division of General Swartzemberg who was left cut off from Minsk and from Beresina. As for me, I continued on my route towards Poland, escorting the carriage of the Count and Countess Vandières, who never ceased to employ the most tender and urgent care for her spouse.

Fleuriot accompanied me. Thus it was we succeeded after a thousand perils, and in the midst of the most cruel privations in reaching the village of Studranzko, which dominated the banks of the Beresina, a river whose name, henceforth, will be written in letters of blood in our history. At Studzranko the horses pulling the Countess's carriage fell expiring in the snow. Fleuriot had also lost his horse, and mine alone remained, but was able to suffice and pull the carriage as far as Vilna. Suddenly we were surrounded by a crowd of refugees, who revived by a huge fire they had just lit, no longer able to endure anything but the need to assuage the hunger they had been prey to for several days. "A horse!" they screamed, noticing the one that remained to us. I wanted to prevent it, I wanted to speak to their hearts of the interest they inspired, and of this woman and the old dying warrior. My threats, my prayers were useless. A shot rang out and this whole famished horde rushed on its prey.

DOCTOR

Ah. What did you do then?

COLONEL

We gave in to necessity, doctor; the danger to Julie, that of the general, gave us new strength, and Fleuriot and I, were able to drag the carriage of the Countess the rest of the way.

DOCTOR (moved, taking his hand)

Ah, my friend.

COLONEL

That's how we reached the bridges of the Beresina. They were being burned, destroyed. Judge my despair. A numberless crowd was waiting on the banks, and Julie, standing on the carriage was staring with a singular expression of terror at this river whose ice floes began to be stained with French blood. Still, the Russians had just seized Studrianka, and their artillery swept the plain. Ney was still keeping them back, but it was necessary to cross the river or fall under the blows of the enemy. "We'll construct a raft," I shouted to this stunned crowd, and at these words a thousand shouts echoed, a thousand arms rose up, trees fell, the wreckage of carts, gun carriages were brought, in less than an hour the work was completed and the raft set afloat. But from the height of the river banks, everyone rushed on it with frightful selfishness. Two places remained and there were three of us—the general, the Countess, and me—because Fleuriot had embarked first to prepare a place for the poor wounded and was unable to make himself heard and return to the shore.

FLEURIOT

"I am giving up my place to you, Colonel," I yelled, trying to pierce the crowd; but my voice was covered by shouts, "Leave! Leave! No! Yes! Wait!"—

It was a storm of human voices.

COLONEL

Your generous offer came to me, Fleuriot, but I couldn't accept it. To save Julie was all my hope! A voice shouted, "Colonel, save the Countess and leave the General—he cannot survive his wounds." A scream of indignation escaped Julie's mouth.

"Choose between us two," yelled the same voice. "My husband! My husband!" she replied with ecstasy! And reviving with new energy, she steadied the shaking feet of the old general, made him get on the raft, and placed herself with him, then turning towards me with eyes full of tears. "Goodbye" she said to me with an accent I'll never forget.

(They rise; Fleuriot picks up the chairs)

The raft was pushed far from the shore, but at that moment a Russian ball struck me in my chest, and I fell, deprived of feeling on the bloody shore.

FLEURIOT

At the same moment, the raft having bumped into the wreckage of the bridge, thirty people were hurled into the Beresina, never to reappear. General Vandières was of that number. The Countess uttered a terrible scream and fainted in my arms. When she woke up, she was mad.

DOCTOR

Horrible catastrophe. Ah, I conceive how this two-fold blow struck the Countess with frightful terror, and how her reason succumbed. But you, my friend, how did you escape?

COLONEL

Saved by the Russians themselves. I was taken to Siberia and I returned to France only after the events of 1814. My first care was to find the Countess. Judge my sorrow to find her deprived of her reason. I appeared before her and I wasn't recognized—only she never stopped saying "Goodbye" in such a touching way, as she had done at the moment of our separation. Then her madness took on a more somber character; she kept repeating in a delirious voice the name of the river that had caused all her misfortunes— Such, Doctor, are the circumstances on which your colleagues in Paris have based the necessity of the experiment we are going to attempt. See if they have correctly judged Madame de Vandières' condition.

DOCTOR

Yes, yes, my friend. Now I approve them—but I won't hide from you that the disturbance must be terrible for the unfortunate woman, for it will be reason or death. But she's young, she's strong, and heaven indeed owes something to those who, like you, have shed their blood for their country.

COLONEL

Ah, my friend, you make me tremble, and in the hope that animates me is recklessly going to—

DOCTOR

I mustn't hide the dangers from you. But I must make you share all my hope. It is more than probable that—

FLEURIOT (low)

Here's the Baron.

COLONEL

That man again.

(Enter the Baron, proud and gay.)

BARON

Gentlemen, gentlemen, you are strangely abusing my patience and my good nature; despite the observations of the family, and to have nothing to reproach myself with, I've brought my ward to the Château fully convinced all the same of the ineffectiveness of your efforts to restore her reason. And, as of yet, I've seen nothing that would make me think— Hurry up, I entreat you, or I'll take my unhappy relative away.

FLEURIOT (aside)

He has an insolent manner.

COLONEL (aside)

The insolent!

BARON

To cure her would render me the happiest of men, unfortunately, I don't believe in miracles. I don't believe in anything at all.

DOCTOR

In that case you are going to be pleasantly surprised. Because, as for me, I believe.

BARON

Truly, Doctor? Brr!

FLEURIOT

There he goes shivering again.

ROSINE (rushing in)

Ah, gentlemen hurry up. The Countess has just experienced a frightful crisis.

COLONEL

What do you mean?

ROSINE

You ordered me to dress her in the clothes she was wearing on the retreat from Moscow, and I had succeeded without much trouble, when suddenly she was attracted to a mirror. She let out a terrible scream and fled towards the park.

COLONEL

Great God! Let's run to find her.

DOCTOR

Come, my friend, come. Now's the time to arm yourself with courage.

TOGETHER (in deep voices)

Let's go, friend. Let hope

Enter into our hearts

And give us confidence

And success and joy,

But silence!

A little prudence!

Yes, my friends,

We are allowed to hope.

Let's go, friend, etc.

(They leave the tent, which soon is folded back and reveals the mock-up of the Beresina with its broken bridges, ice, and banks covered with dead bodies.)

JULIE (rushing in in confusion)

Snow—frosty, cold—Winter! Oh, I'm cold, I remember I was cold then. But I wasn't alone. There were three of us. Always three. Him there and him here. Now I am alone. And I'm cold again. Oh, quite cold.

COLONEL (returning followed by the Doctor.)

There she is! There she is!

DOCTOR

Let's watch her carefully.

JULIE (seeing the fire on the left)

Oh—fire—fire.

(running to it and kneeling by the fire.) Oh, how good it is. I still remember. Other fires, lots of fires, shining in the plain. They were everywhere! And I was listening with pleasure to the songs from a neighboring bivouac.

COLONEL (to Doctor)

It's the eve of the battle of Smolensk.

DOCTOR

Her memories are coming back.

JULIE

Grenadier, if you want to sing something else. Tell him—who was there. Oh, pardon, officer. I didn't see the Countess. The Countess? That was me. Yes, that was me. And it seems to me I still hear the Grenadier's song.

(sings)

To make the ice blow up

Fires aren't worth a tender shoot.

Tiraliralira!

Goodbye! Goodbye!

DOCTOR

Come, my friend, it's time to strike the final blow.

(he pulls the Colonel off. Somber music.)

JULIE (rising with a scream of terror)

Ah! How everything has changed. No more songs. No more bread. No more fire. No—more—sleep everywhere. And me, I'm dozing, too. And yet a voice is constantly shouting at me. "Julie! Julie! Julie! Don't sleep here. Sleep is death." Never mind. I want to sleep.

(she kneels)

VOICES (Confused and distant)

Long live the Emperor!

JULIE (assuming a new energy and rising.)

The Emperor! Ah, there he is passing by on horseback. Long live the Emperor! He's crossing the bridge. He's saved! He's going to see France again, he is! But the others. They are dead, too. The one who was there and the one who was here! Who's he? Who?

(she rubs her face)

Oh, my God! He's no more than a name for me.

(cannon fire can be heard)

Ah, the war, the war!

(she listens attentive, eyes haggard, mouth wide open.)

SOLDIERS (pitifully scaling a ravine.)

O poor France

See the suffering

Of your wandering soldiers.

Dying.

What misery

Pursues your children

On this earth.

Soldiers, Frenchmen—that misery overwhelms.

Speak! Where are you coming from?

SOLDIERS

We are coming from Moscow..

JULIE

From Moscow, Shocking reversal.

SOLDIERS

What a disaster for us. But, frightful sight. What river is that?

JULIE (singing)

It's the Beresina.

SOLDIERS (moving away)

O poor France, etc.

JULIE

The Beresina. Ah, yes, the Beresina. And the Count de Vandières? Ah, over there, wounded, expiring. My friend, my friend, courage. There. The banks of the Beresina you know. But I am with you. Lean on my arm. Come, come—

FLEURIOT (in the distance)

Colonel. Get to the raft. The Russians are here.

JULIE (terrified)

The Russians.

COLONEL (appearing)

Save the Countess de Vandières.

JULIE

Save the General! Goodbye! Goodbye!

(the Russians appear on the heights. A shot rings out.)

COLONEL (feigning being wounded)

Ah! Julie! Julie!

JULIE (with a scream)

Ah, him, him! Falbert! Falbert!

(She tries to run to him but stumbles and falls. Seeing Julie fall, the Doctor, together with the Colonel rush to help her. Valets bring up an armchair and help her to sit. She remains inanimate. Worry and confusion is depicted on her face.)

CHORUS (in deep voices)

Terror, hope

Agitate me in turn

No question her suffering

Will end without return.

(The music continues, Julie comes to herself gently. Calm returns to all faces.)

JULIE

Where am I? What terrifying dream has just ended for me? It seems to me I'm reborn to life. Yes, my soul's awakening. It's me, it's really me. And him, Ah, Falbert!

DOCTOR

She's saved. Bravo!

BARON (shivering)

Brr!

FLEURIOT (aside)

Now he's no longer trembling, he's choking.

BARON (aside)

Something to hang myself with.

FLEURIOT (hearing him, cheerfully)

I'm not opposed to that.

COLONEL

Dear Julie, you've finally come back to me, Ah, if you could read in my heart.

JULIE (recognizing them)

Rosine, Fleuriot, good doctor. (with terror) The Baron!

BARON

My dear sister—I'm ravished.

JULIE (sadly)

Ah, poor Vandières! Dead! Down there. Before my eyes, in the waves. (with dignity) Yet one more year for the memory of the general and the rest of my life—for you.

GENERAL CHORUS

Happy moment!

Finally, no more torment;

Because this fortunate day

Returns her to his love.

Sweet pleasures and grandeur

All seem to return

To embellish

His future.

CURTAIN

THE END OF MURAT
BY JEAN BERLEUX AND ALEXANDRE DUMAS

CAST OF CHARACTERS

MURAT

GENERAL NUNZIANTE

TAVELLA, former Sergeant

PELLEGRINO

TRENTA CAPELLI, Captain of Gendarmes

CAPTAIN STRATI

LA CAMERA, Crown Attorney

ANTONIO DE MASAIDA, priest

GENERAL FRANCESCHETTI

CAMPANA, Murat's aide-de-camp

CONCIERGE OF THE PRISON

LIEUTENANT

FRANCESCA

Tailor, Soldiers, Gendarmes, Prisoners, Inhabitants of Pizzo

AUTHOR'S PREFACE

I was profoundly struck as I read *Captain Arena* by Alexandre Dumas, by the dramatic description of the execution of Murat. It seemed to me one could easily bring it to the stage. Mr. Alexandre Dumas, Fils, having graciously granted me authorization, I applied myself to putting it on stage, with the least possible change; that's why I have used the very text of Alexandre Dumas as dialogue in whole passages, principally in the second scene. Only the episode of Francesca belongs to me; I thought it was necessary to strengthen the action. As for the rest, I leave the responsibility of historic documents to my illustrious deceased collaborator.

—June 1890

SCENE I

The Action takes place in Pizzo, from 8 to 13 October, 1815.

The Square of Pizzo, October 8, 1815. A confusion of Italian houses, mostly single story. To the left, a statue of King Ferdinand. Four tortuous sloping streets lead into the square. At the back of the stage a great stairway hewn from granite runs down to the sea, which can be perceived very blue in the distance. At rise, the church bell rings, calling the faithful to Mass. The peasants leave their homes, men, women, and children, heading in groups, all on the same side, to the left of the stage, passing before the statue of King Ferdinand. They wear the costumes of Neapolitan fishermen. A rolling of drums echoes in the distance, followed by the indistinct voice of a public crier. One hears briefly parts of phrases such as, "Rebel", "Joachim"—"price on his head." Some peasants stop to listen. Soon a group forms.

PELLEGRINO (orating in the midst of the group)

Do you hear? It's the usurper who's got a price on it. Is

he to be found in the country?

A PEASANT

Possibly. I went to Cosenza yesterday. All they were talking of was him. They said how he came from Corsica with an army. There were police everywhere. Captain Trenta Capelli arrived here yesterday evening. He slept at his uncle Mattei's. I saw him this morning.

ANOTHER PEASANT

Without doubt they're going to go fight again.

PELLEGRINO

If the usurper comes to Pizzo, I know someone who will settle his hash.

FIRST PEASANT

We will never be calm in this ragamuffin country.

A WOMAN

He is, it seems, a handsome man, King Joachim.

ANOTHER WOMAN

You didn't see him when he came here five years ago.

FRANCESCA (approaching)

You speak idly. He was a good king. In his times things were happy, and he wasn't proud to the poor of the world. Whoever wanted to could approach him, right, Tavella?

TAVELLA

Indeed, it's true. I served in his guard. I was a sergeant. He spoke to me twice.

PELLEGRINO

Yes, but King Ferdinand is the real legitimate King. The other one is only a usurper imposed by the French.

FRANCESCA

A usurper who was better than the legitimate king.

YOUNG GIRL (to Francesca)

As for you, we know quite well you would never speak ill of him. (to the others) She's in love.

FRANCESCA (blushing)

Oh!

YOUNG GIRL

Everyone knows quite well. Go on: since he came to Pizzo, you've been unable to eat or drink.

PELLEGRINO (to Francesca)

Well, if your lover returns—we'll cut his throat. (more laughter)

TAVELLA

Believe me, Pellegrino, if that should happen the best thing would be for everyone to stay at home. It's not for us poor devils to busy ourselves with kings. We always get skinned. I am older than you, and I've seen some revolutions. Let the storm pass. For the vanquished today may be the victor tomorrow. And then it's always the peasants who pay—

PELLEGRINO

Never mind; if Joachim returns to the throne, there will be another war.

A WOMAN

War—Good Madonna! Yet another war!

TAVELLA

For sure. We don't want any more war.

FRANCESCA

That's not good for an old soldier like you to speak like that, Tavella.

A PEASANT

Shut up! We've had enough war. You're right, Tavella.

ALL

It's true— We've had enough of it.

WOMAN

As for me, I lost my husband in the war.

AN OLD PEASANT

And as for me, my only son.

FRANCESCA

Why did King Joachim make war?

PELLEGRINO

Does anyone know? For nothing, as always to imitate these Satanic French. He will be at it again, to find his Napoleon of ill luck.

A PEASANT

Down with war!

ALL

Yes, yes—down with war.

A CHILD (to Tavella, and pointing to the sea)

Look there, Father, look there. That big ship—and the small boat is approaching the shore.

TAVELLA

Where? By Jove, it's true. Look, all of you. There are people disembarking.

(All turn towards the back of the stage looking in the direction of the large stairway.)

CHILD

Hold on—there they are—coming up.

(They appear at the top of the stairs, Murat is in the lead, dressed in a blue suit adorned with gold at the neck, on his chest, and on his pockets. He is wearing pants of white cashmere, boots for riding, a belt through which is passed a brace of pistols; a hat braided with gold like his suit, decorated with white, and whose cord is made of fourteen blazing diamonds. At the arrival of the small troop the peasants draw back bit by bit, manifesting signs of astonishment.)

FRANCESCA (recognizing Murat)

Lord Jesus, it's him.

MURAT (pointing out Tavella to Campana who is behind him)

By Jove, Luck favors us. Don't you recognize that man, Campana? It's a former sergeant of my Guard. (going straight to Tavella and setting his hand on his shoulder) Your name's Tavella?

TAVELLA

Yes. What do you want from me?

MURAT

Tavella, don't you recognize me? (Travella remains mute) Tavella, I am Joachim Murat, your former general. The honor goes to you of being the first to shout, "Long Live, Joachim!"

(Franceschetti, Campana, and Murat's partisans shout, "Long Live Joachim!" Murmurs amongst the peasants. Not one has responded to the shouting "Long Live Joachim!" Pellegrino sneaks out to the left.)

MURAT

Tavella, go find me a horse, and from being Sergeant, I will make you Captain. (Tavella moves away without answering. New, muffled murmurs amongst the peasants.)

GENERAL FRANCESCHETTI (approaching)

Sire, what must be done?

MURAT

Do you think that man will bring me a horse?

FRANCESCHETTI

Sire, I don't think so.

MURAT

In that case, let's go on foot to Monteleone.

CAMPANA

Sire, it would, perhaps, be more prudent to return to the shore.

MURAT

It's too late the dice are already cast. Let my destiny be accomplished! To Monteleone.

SOLDIERS

To Monteleone! (Murat and his partisans leave.)

(Trenta Capelli in the uniform of a Captain of Gendarmes and Pellegrino armed with a rifle enter.)

PELLEGRINO

Here, Captain they've just left from here.

TRENTA CAPELLI

Fine. (addressing the peasants) Friends, will you allow a conspirator to dirty the soil of the country? A usurper who brings you civil war?

PEASANTS

No, no.

TRENTA CAPELLI

You know there are a thousand crowns for whoever captures him. (Diverse murmurs. Shouts, "To arms!")

PEASANTS

To arms! To arms! (The peasants run to their houses and return almost immediately with their rifles and their cartridge pouches, which they hastily secure and fasten.) Let's run to pursue them. That way, Captain—

they went that way.

TRENTA CAPELLI

Follow me.

PELLEGRINO

That's unnecessary. Here they are coming back.

(Trenta Capelli, noticing Murat, signals the peasants to remain behind. He advances alone and addresses Murat)

TRENTA CAPELLI

Your retreat is cut off. We are thirty against one. Surrender and spare the shedding of blood.

MURAT

I have something better to offer you. Follow me—join with me: there are epaulettes of general for you, and for each of the men, fifty Napoleons.

TRENTA CAPELLI

What you propose to me is impossible; we are devoted to King Ferdinand—in life and in death. You cannot doubt it. Not one of them responded to your shout of "Long Live Joachim!" did they? Listen. (raising his sword) "Long live Ferdinand!"

PEASANTS

Long Live Ferdinand!

MURAT

It will be as God wishes, but I will not surrender.

TRENTA CAPELLI

Then let the blood fall on those who shed it. (Pellegrino aims at Murat)

MURAT

Step aside, Captain. You're preventing this man from aiming at me. (Trenta Capelli rushes aside; the shot is fired but misses Murat)

MURAT (low to Franceschetti and Campana)

The game is lost. Let's try to get back to our ship. (The soldiers protect Murat as they fall back to the stairway. Confusion.)

(The whole population runs in pursuit of Murat shouting, "Death!" The stage empties and remains empty. Murmurs can be heard that ever increase. Then rifle shots. First spaced, then more. One feels that a real battle is taking place near the sea. Finally shouts of triumph succeed screams of death. Then one sees Murat reappear surrounded by peasants who strike him, shouting at him. His suit is in shreds, his epaulettes have been torn off, his face is covered with blood. The entire population of Pizzo is stampeding into the royal quarry, women more enraged than the men. Pellegrino is seen amongst the most excited. Trenta Capelli and the gendarmes make vain efforts to protect Murat. Francesca is alone on the side of the stage that remains empty. She falls to her knees.)

FRANCESCA

Holy Madonna, protect the King!

(Murat is dragged before the statue of Ferdinand. There, the howling increases.)

CURTAIN

SCENE II

A room with walls whitewashed with lime, and covered with a multitude of images of Madonnas and Saints as found in most Italian homes. A wooden table and some straw chairs compose the furnishings. At the back, a low wooden, sculpted chest on which are placed small objects; an inkwell and sheets of paper. Above the chest a mirror hangs suspended. Door to the left. To the right an iron bed on which Murat is stretched dressed in the uniform of a Neapolitan officer. He is sleeping restlessly. Little by little he wakes up.

MURAT (waking up)

Did I dream? It seems to me that I was sleeping deeply. Yes, indeed, it's a dream I just had the dream of my entire life. Was this me I was seeing again just now? Me, the son of an innkeeper become a general, Marshal of the Empire, Prince, Grand Admiral, great eagle of the Legion of Honor, Grand Duke of Cleves and Berg—King, King and brother-in-law of Napoleon! Napoleon! Ah! Why did that thought come to assail me again? Why does it come to reproach me for having betrayed you, Napoleon, in my mad ambition to preserve this fallen throne that you let me pick up from the flap of your imperial mantle! Twice I compounded with your enemies; and that will be the remorse of my entire life. The only bad memory which raises itself before me—at the moment of my death. (discouraged) Come on, let's forget, if it can be forgotten. (dreaming again) Mondovi! Saint Georges! Marengo! Egypt and the sparkling Mamelukes! The Pyramids! Saint-Jean d'Acre! Aboukir! Jena! Eylau! Friedland! Oh beautiful battles, beautiful cavalry charges! Great blows with the sabre! Smolensk! Moscow! And everywhere the snow was falling, enveloping the army in a cold winding sheet. (taking his head in his hand and sighing) Alas! That I wasn't at Waterloo! Pardon, Napoleon, pardon, my brother. You, so good, so generous, so great. You that through my sin, they've nailed on that rocky desert so as to make an apotheosis of sorrows and tears for the most prodigious man that ever existed. (silence) How much glory and how much misery. And all this to terminate in the end like an adventurer, ignominiously shot by an unruly soldiery in the pay of some despot in the back of some low gully. Never mind: I will know how to die. They shall not be able to say that one who risked his life in a hundred battles feared death for a moment. Since I've been unable to recapture my kingdom, since I've lost, I will pay—that's all. (feverishly he walks back and forth for a few minutes, then comes to sit back down on the bed. The sound of steps can be heard.) There's my executioner. (standing proudly) Away with discouragement! We shall become

King Joachim again. (the door opens and the Concierge timidly approaches Murat) What is it? What do they want with me?

CONCIERGE

Sire, these are the clothes Your Majesty ordered the day before yesterday. The tailor is here.

MURAT

That's fine; let him bring them. (the Tailor enters) Ah, it's you. I thought you would never finish! This uniform weighs on me. (bitterly) A uniform with Ferdinand's colors. But they had put me in such a state. (the Tailor unfolds the package he has bought. He extracts from it a dark blue coat, trimmed with rich brocades, of the same shade, but brighter than all the needlework. The vest is white, striped with amaranth, the pants of white cashmere, equally brocaded in gold.)

MURAT (with satisfaction)

Perfect! They couldn't have done better in Paris! (placing his arm into the sleeve, then the coat. Turns around, making an effort to twist) Not even a mirror to see oneself! Ah! that mirror. (looking at himself in the mirror—arranging the neck with his hand, then to the Tailor) See, the neck is a bit high. But that will be good enough for a few days. Wait here—there should also be a correction. But never mind. (with an air of nonchalance) For this once, I will put up with it.

TAILOR

Your Excellency is satisfied?

MURAT

(haughtily) Call me, Majesty. I am your king. (tossing him a purse) Pay yourself.

TAILOR (stammering)

Yes, Sire—pardon, Majesty. At your orders, Sire. (leaves, bowing to the ground.)

CONCIERGE

Does Your Majesty desire supper? (Murat gives a gesture of assent. The Concierge brings in a cold chicken, bread, a bottle of wine, etc.)

CONCIERGE

Does Your Majesty wish to receive General Nunziante?

MURAT

Let him enter. (starts eating) Leave us.

(The Concierge leaves; Murat is seated at the table eating; General Nunziante enters.)

MURAT

It's you, General. Would you like to dine with me? I'm as hungry as an ogre. Damn! It's not a meal fit for a king that I am offering you. But Damn! War is war. There were days in my life as a soldier when I ate worse than today. That's agreed. Sit down.

GENERAL (sadly)

I thank Your Majesty, but I've just had supper.

MURAT

Well, sit down all the same. We will chat, what the devil! I can't tell you what pleasure I have chatting with you. (The General sits but remains mute. Murat speaks, as he eats) Why, by Jove! What a face you're making. You have an irritating communication to make? Speak quickly, for the three days I've lived in this cursed room, I've received nothing but bad news. Aside from the chicken which is excellent, and the good bath I took yesterday, thanks to you, I rarely find myself so ill. So you can speak in confidence. I am prepared for it. (The General hesitates and stammers.) Well, well, you seem upset. Let's bet it's a dispatch from Ferdinand that you have to communicate to me?

GENERAL

Yes, Sire.

MURAT

Give it, give it quickly. (The General hands him a parchment) The Devil! a decree—an official one. (opens it, reads) Ferdinand, by the grace of God, etc. etc. Let's keep going— Ah, I am there. Having decreed and decree as follows Article 1. General Murat will be tried by a military commission whose members will be selected by our Minister of War. Article 2. There will be granted to the condemned only a half hour to receive the comforts of religion— At least that's clear. It's quite simply my execution that this good brother has decreed. He so little doubts his judges that he has regulated the time that must elapse between my condemnation and my death. That's expeditious. And who are the members of this tribunal of assassins? (reading) The Crown Attorney La Camera, Lieutenant Francesco Frozo, Captain Strati, etc. (continuing to read, low) Better and better; admirable! Not even a general.

GENERAL

Sire, Captain Strati is here and desires to speak to Your Majesty. He asks to be admitted and waits for you to give the order. (Murat rises and gives a sign that the Captain can enter.)

MURAT (aside)

Now I understand this General's embarrassment.

CAPTAIN STRATI (approaching Murat)

General, I am charged with informing you of the directive of the trial commission. Here it is. The tribunal has just assembled at this very moment. My mission is to ask you if you will follow me to appear there.

MURAT (with a smile on his lips)

Never, sir, never! (scornfully, and little by little becoming animated) Go tell those improvised judges—your colleagues, that I do not recognize, and will never recognize a tribunal composed of simple officers. If they wish to treat me as a king, I must be judged by a tribunal of kings; if they wish to treat me as a Marshal of France, I demand a commission of Marshals. Finally, if they wish to treat me as a general, and (bitterly) it seems to me I have some right to that, the least they can do is to assemble a jury of generals. For me to descend to the level of judges who've just been named, too many pages must be torn off the history of Europe. As for now, I refuse to recognize the legality of the tribunal which is imposed on me.

CAPTAIN STRATI

It's not given to me to reply to your questions, General; my duty was to communicate to you the order which is here; discipline requires me to do it, I've done it. I beg Your Excellency to willingly pardon me.

MURAT (with animation)

That's all right, sir, that's all right. Anyway, it's not on any of you that the odious crime you are committing will fall back on; it will fall back on Ferdinand, who will have treated one of his brothers as he would treat a brigand. Tell the commission that it can proceed without me. I will not submit to the tribunal whatever happens, and if I am brought there by force, I swear to God that no human power will be able to make me break silence.

CAPTAIN STRATI

Your Excellency will at least be willing to give me his name, age, and place of birth?

MURAT (haughtily)

I am Joachim Napoleon, King of the Two Sicilies, born at Bastide-Fortunière, in France, and history will add, assassinated in Pizzo. Now that you know what you wished to know, I order you to leave.

(Captain Strati bows and leaves.)

(Murat strides up and down in prey to an unutterable exaltation. Little by little he softens and addresses the General.)

MURAT

Here's a dinner singularly interrupted. I let myself get a bit carried away, it's true—but you will admit it was caused by too much impudence.

GENERAL

Still, Sire—

MURAT

What, you too, General, you who I knew formerly, you that I even, and still do consider as a friend? You would advise me—? Never, you hear, never will I present myself to a tribunal of traitors and regicides. And no one in the world can make me reverse my determination.

(A silence.)

GENERAL

Your Majesty will permit me to retire?

MURAT

What, you are abandoning me? Why, no—I understand your thought. You want to go down there and bring me news as soon as you have any. Thanks, my friend, thanks. (He offers his hand; the General grasps it, bows, and leaves.)

MURAT (alone)

It's finished; they are going to condemn me. That's certain, since they've been ordered to do it. Well, Murat, you will know how to die. (dreaming) Such a well planned expedition. Everything was ready. I had money, men. Why did it happen that chance brought me to throw myself into this little village. Everywhere else, I would have been acclaimed. And without that infamous Barbara who abandoned me in such a cowardly way, doubtless to steal the treasure that I had confided to him, I would have regained my ship. But it's always necessary to slip in a traitor somewhere to baffle the best-laid plans. (with disgust) That's humanity. (Sits on his bed, a prey to his thoughts.)

(The door opens softly. The Concierge appears—then he lets Francesca enter.)

CONCIERGE

Go, my child, and may God permit you to succeed. (he leaves and locks the door. At that sound, Murat raises his head.)

MURAT

What is it now? (noticing Francesca with surprise) A young girl. (good naturedly) Approach, child.

FRANCESCA (throwing herself on her knees before Murat)

Sire, sire, pardon my audacity—but it's for Your Majesty's good that I dare approach you.

MURAT (rising)

Speak child, I am listening to you.

FRANCESCA

Sire, my name is Francesca. I am the daughter of the man who guards this house. But weak woman though I am, I think that I could be useful to Your Majesty. Sire, my father is devoted to you; he's never dared to speak to you of our plans, and he's made me responsible for doing that. Sire, if you consent, and if it pleases God, tonight you will be free.

MURAT (with an explosion of joy)

Ah, there are still brave people on this earth!

FRANCESCA

Here's what Your Majesty must do. When everyone's gone to bed, when there's no one else around to watch except the sentinels who are guarding you, my father will bring me here as he just did. Let Your Majesty change clothes with me; no one will be suspicious seeing a woman leave. By shaving your whiskers, by carefully dissimulating your voice, by stooping slightly, they will take you for me. Once out of the prison, my father will escort you to the beach. There a boatman that we've won over will be waiting for you; you will get into his ship and you will reach Corsica without danger.

MURAT (listens attentively; little by little his features become more somber as he speaks to the young girl)

All this is very well contrived; but you, my child, do you know that it's death waiting for you?

FRANCESCA

I know it.

MURAT

Have you carefully considered?

FRANCESCA

I've carefully considered.

MURAT

Then why do you want to die? What have I done to inspire you with such self-sacrifice?

FRANCESCA (excitedly)

Nothing, nothing, Sire— May Your Majesty pardon me!

MURAT

Still, it's a crime to want to die so young. Don't you love anybody then? (Francesca shivers and makes a negative gesture) But your father? How can he authorize such a sacrifice?

FRANCESCA

My father once served under Your Majesty at the time you were winning so many battles. A simple soldier, it is not surprising that Your Majesty didn't recognize him. He wasn't like Tavella, who was a sergeant. At the crossing of the Beresina, when the bridge was collapsing under the weight of the army, you were on the other shore and you extended your hand to a drowning man. You don't remember it, without doubt, Sire—you saved so many people that day! That man was my father; he owes you his life. Today it is I who will pay his debt, that's all.

MURAT

And you consented, my child?

FRANCESCA

Oh, me! Alas! Sire, nothing attaches me to life. (with subdued passion) I will be so happy to save you. (Murat gestures in astonishment) Sire, it was five years ago Your Majesty came to Pizzo. You came by the high road from Cosenza and the whole village was there to see you pass. That day, you see, Sire, has remained graven in my memory. You were in a fine uniform, quite resplendent with gold, surrounded by an escort of sparkling officers; the sky was blue with a beautiful sun, as if the weather wanted to celebrate you. Everyone shouted, "Long Live the King! Long Live Joachim!" And you were so handsome, so handsome on your big, black, prancing horse. Why, you would have said an archangel had descended from paradise. Alas, all that happened so quickly! I am only a poor peasant girl, Sire, but the other day when I saw you beaten, mistreated, torn apart by those same people who formerly acclaimed you, when I learned they intended to shoot you, I thought that Your Majesty would not reject me, and I came, naturally, to put myself at your service, very happy, if necessary, to give my life and liberty for that of my King.

MURAT

Nice, little one, nice.

FRANCESCA (begging, almost wheedling)

So you accept! You really want to, speak?

MURAT

Certainly not; I refuse. (aside) It shall not be said that a child paid with her head the ransom of my life.

FRANCESCA (throwing herself at his feet)

Sire, from pity, from pity, permit me to save you. (Murat tries to raise her, but she clings desperately to him. In anguish, losing her head) I don't want it! I don't want for you to die!

MURAT (appears very surprised by this insistence; he seems to meditate for a moment while Francesca, breathlessly awaits his reply)

Well, so be it, I accept. (aside) There will still be time to undeceive her. (aloud) Tonight, I will be ready. (raising her up, with kindness) Well?—are you satisfied?

FRANCESCA (passionately)

Thanks, thanks, my King.

MURAT

Until this evening. (stopping her as she heads toward the door) What? Are you running off like that? Now, you'd say I frighten you. At least before leaving me, you will allow me to embrace you, child.

FRANCESCA (radiant, stammering)

Sire—sire. (she offers him her face on which Murat plants a kiss.) That kiss, Sire, will remain always graven here and here. (pointing in exaltation to her face and her heart. At the door she says to her father who comes to open for her—with an explosion of joy) He accepts, father, he accepts! (she leaves)

MURAT

Dear child—Generous heart! Rare soul. Ah, that makes up for so much shame. (pulling from his pocket a watch studded with gems on its lid a miniature of the Queen. He kisses it longingly) Soon, three o'clock. What are my judges doing? It seems to be a lengthy deliberation. (as he returns his watch to his pocket, his eyes rest on the portrait of the Queen) Dear wife! How it really resembles you! (sighing) Here, perhaps, are the only two sincere affections that I've had in my life. My beloved Caroline and this little girl who left me. (dries a tear) Caroline! My Caroline! I want to address a last goodbye to you before dying. (takes ink and paper on the chest at the back of the stage, places it on a corner of the table which hasn't even been cleaned up, and starts to write. When he finishes the letter, he reads aloud) "Dear Caroline of my heart: The fatal hour has come. I am going to die. The extreme penalty. In a few hours you will no longer have a spouse and our children will no longer have a father; remember me and don't ever forget my memory. I am dying innocent and my life is being taken by an unjust judgment. Goodbye, my Achilles, goodbye, my dear Suzanne, goodbye, my Lucien, goodbye, my Louise. Show yourselves worthy of me; I am leaving you a land and a kingdom full of my enemies. Show yourselves superior to adversity and remember not to believe yourself more than you are when thinking of what you have been. Goodbye, I bless you. Never curse my memory. Remember that the greatest sorrow I am experiencing in my sacrifice is that I am dying far from my children, far from my wife, and not having any friend to shut my eyes. Goodbye, my Caroline. Goodbye, my children, receive my paternal benediction, my tender caresses, and my last kisses. Goodbye, goodbye, and never forget your wretched father." (two large tears roll down the length of Murat's cheeks. Someone knocks discreetly at the door. Murat dries his tears and resumes a calm face) Come in! (General Nunziante enters. Murat goes to him excitedly) Well, what General? (The General silently lowers his head) Death, right? (The General makes an affirmative gesture. Proudly) I was expecting it.

GENERAL

Here's the Crown Attorney, who will give you a report of his mission.

(The Crown Attorney, La Camera, enters, holding The

Commission's judgment in his hand.)

MURAT

Read, sir, I am listening to you.

LA CAMERA (reading)

"The Military Commission—convened at ten o'clock on the morning of the 13th day of this month of October, 1815, in the Castle of Pizzo to Judge the French General Joachim Murat—"

MURAT (haughtily)

Say, King, sir—

LA CAMERA (continuing)

"Considering the reading of the laws, the examination of the witnesses, and the result of the discussion have given rise to establish that Murat attempted to destroy the government, to incite the citizens to take up arms against the King and the public order, to introduce a revolt into the Commune of Pizzo, and to extend it throughout the realm—which constitutes him culpable of an outrage against the internal security of the state and public enemy—Considering, that these outrages were foreseen by articles 87 and 94 of the penal code—"

MURAT

Why, that law—it was I who made it!

LA CAMERA

"The Commission has decided unanimously that the provisions of these articles are applicable to Joachim Murat. From these considerations and with the same unanimity has condemned him and does condemn him to the penalty of death with confiscation of his property. IT IS ORDERED That the present judgment shall be executed diligently by the reporter. PRONOUNCED at two o'clock in the afternoon on the said day, month, and year above."

MURAT (rising and addressing La Camera)

Is that all, sir?

LA CAMERA

General, I hope that you will die without any feeling of animosity against us, and that you do not exempt yourself from the law that you yourself made.

MURAT

Sir, I made that law for brigands and not for crowned heads.

LA CAMERA

The law is equal for all, sir.

MURAT

That may be, when it is useful to certain people; but whoever has been a King bears with him a sacred character which would require one to think twice before treating him as just anybody. I honored King Ferdinand by thinking he would not shoot me like a criminal. I was mistaken; so much the worse for him; Let's not discuss it any further. As for wishing you ill, I don't hold it any more against you than a common soldier who, in the midst of a skirmish, having received from his leader the order to fire at me, sends a bullet through my body. Go, sir—and may God keep you in his holy and worthy care. (Murat pronounces these last words, smiling. As soon as the Crown Attorney leaves, he approaches General Nunziante.) General, I have a great service to ask of you. Here's a letter addressed to my beloved wife, Queen Caroline. Give me your word that this letter will be delivered. Ah, and then (playfully) there's a child here, a young girl who interests me. She's the daughter of the guard of this house; her name's Francesca, I think; here's a ring I desire to leave her as a memory of my captivity. Do you promise me, general, that this ring will be delivered to this child, and my letter to my wife?

GENERAL (turning away to hide his emotion)

I swear it to you.

MURAT (patting him on the shoulder)

Well, well, general! What's this? What the devil! We are both soldiers—we've looked death in the face. I am going to see it again, that's all, and this time it will come at my directive, which is not always the case. For I hope they will allow me to order the firing, won't they? (The General nods his head.)

MURAT

Now, general. What time is set for my execution?

GENERAL

Sire, designate it yourself.

MURAT

I don't intend to make you wait.

GENERAL

I hope you don't think that's the motive—

MURAT

Come on, General, I am joking. (pulls out his watch,

looks at the portrait of Queen Caroline, then hands it to the General.) Look, General. How it resembles the Queen. (ready to put it back in his pocket.) Ah! Pardon, I was forgetting the principal thing. It is past three; it will be for four o'clock, if you like. Fifty-five minutes is too much?

GENERAL

That's fine, Sire. (starts to leave)

MURAT

Will I not see you again?

GENERAL

My instructions are that I will be present at your execution; but I don't know if I have the strength.

MURAT

That's fine, that's fine, child that you are. (General Nunziante rushes towards the door, ready to burst into tears. He bumps into a priest, Don Antonio de Masaida. A tall old man with a respectable face, grave demeanor, and simple manners. Murat notices the priest.) What does this man want with me? Does he think I have need of his exhortations, and that I don't know how to die?

GENERAL

He asks to enter, Sire.

MURAT

Well—let him enter! (General Nunziante leaves.) Now, what do you want! I'm going to be shot in three-quarters of an hour and I have no time to waste.

PRIEST

Sire, I'm coming to ask if you wish to die as a Christian?

MURAT

I will die as a soldier. (The Priest doesn't budge.) Didn't you hear me, father?

PRIEST

You didn't receive me this way the first time you saw me, Sire. It's true that in those days you were King and I came to ask you a favor.

MURAT

Indeed. Your face is not unfamiliar to me. Where then have I seen you?

PRIEST

Right here, Sire. When you came to Pizzo in 1810, I asked you for assistance in completing our church: twenty-five thousand francs. You gave me forty thousand.

MURAT (smiling)

That's because I foresaw I would be buried there.

PRIEST

Well, Sire, will you refuse an old man the last request he asks of you?

MURAT

Which is?

PRIEST

That of dying like a Christian.

MURAT

You want me to confess in the past I disobeyed my father who didn't want me to be a soldier. That's the only thing I repent of. The rest concerns only myself.

PRIEST

But, Sire, would you give me a testimonial that you are dying in the Catholic faith?

MURAT

Oh—without difficulty. (sits down and scribbles a letter which he reads aloud.) "I, Joachim Murat, die as a Christian believing in the Holy Roman Catholic Apostolic Church." (gives the letter to the Priest. After seeming to hesitate) Father, your blessing.

PRIEST

With all my heart. (places his hands on Murat's head bowed head; murmuring like a priest.)

MURAT

Goodbye, Father.

PRIEST

Goodbye, my son. (The Priest leaves.)

MURAT (alone)

That man made me lose precious time. Forty minutes remain. That's hardly sufficient to make oneself handsome for death. (puts on his clothes, goes to the mirror, and begins smoothing his hair.)

CURTAIN

SCENE III

A courtyard. On the left a straight staircase between two walls that forms a sort of hollow on the stage. At the back of the stage, the wall of a house, adjoining to the right the prison of the condemned petty criminals. In the middle of the prison a latticed window closed with large iron bars. Through the bars appear the heads of the curious. These are the prisoners who press themselves, attracted by the unusual noises of preparations, uneasy about what is going to take place. Beneath the window a squad of six infantrymen commanded by a lieutenant with a drummer. At rise, a roll of drums. A silence. A low door piercing the wall of the house facing the audience opens. Murat comes out, followed by General Nunziante. Quarter after four strikes. Murat is garbed in the outfit brought by the Tailor in Scene II. His head is naked; his dark hair carefully parted over his face. One can guess that much of the time that remained to him has been spent on his toilet.

MURAT (in the doorway, addressing General Nunziante)

General, you're late. (At Murat's entry an uproar behind

the prisoners window.)

PRISONERS

It's King Joachim? Are they going to shoot him? Move aside a bit so I can see. Yie! You're hurting me. It's really him! I recognize him. Don't push so hard, you're squashing me. (at the uproar, the Lieutenant who commands the firing squad looks up.)

LIEUTENANT

Shut up! Goddamnit!

(The uproar stops, persisting in murmurs which last throughout the entire scene. Murat advances with a firm step; then taking a theatrical pose which he affects, stands boldly in front of the soldiers.)

MURAT (to the soldiers in a firm voice)

My friends, the court is straight enough for you to fire accurately. Aim for the chest, spare my face. (turning towards the General) Goodbye, General—and thanks for all you have done for me.

(General Nunziante, overwhelmed by emotion cannot find a word to say, and kisses Murat's hands which he abandons to him.)

MURAT (calmly, without rushing, goes to place himself in the hollow formed by the stairway, then mounting the steps, he addresses the soldiers anew)

My friends—

(New exclamations by the prisoners behind the window.)

PRISONERS

How handsome he is! That's because he's not afraid! He's less pale than the general. Shut up! Listen to him.

LIEUTENANT

Goddamnit! will you shut up! (turning to Murat) Swine, General, condemned to prison.

MURAT (with kindness)

Let them look, since they want to see. But I recognize them. I was locked up with them the day of my arrest. Poor Devils! I believe they remember me because I left them some money.

PRISONERS

It's true, it's true. I still have a gold piece.

MURAT

Well! Silence I beg you. This won't be long and later you can tell how you saw a King die! (the uproar ceases. To the soldiers in a thrilling voice) Platoon! Arms! Aim! Fire!

(Three shots only are fired; one after the other. Murat remains standing impassively. Not a muscle in his face has budged. General Nunziante and the Lieutenant look at each other in consternation. Murmurs in the prisoners cell.)

MURAT (to soldiers)

Thanks, comrades. But that's useless. Let's start over again, and no mercy, I beg you.

(At this moment Francesca appears at the top of the stairs.)

FRANCESCA

My God! My God!

MURAT (in a tone of command)

Load in double time. Load your weapons. Aim! Fire!

(Firing. Murat rolls face to the ground.)

FRANCESCA

Oh! The cowards! The cowards! (she faints)

LIEUTENANT

Port Arms! Shoulder Arms! By the right flank! March!

(The Curtain falls slowly as the soldiers execute the Lieutentant's commands, and as General Nunziante heads towards Murat's cadaver.)

CURTAIN

THE TRIAL OF MARSHAL NEY

BY LOUIS-MARIE FONTAN AND CHARLES DUPEUTY

CAST OF CHARACTERS

Marshal Ney

A General

Bellart, Procurer-General

Count Laujuinais

Duke de Richelieu

Duke of Wellington

President of the Chamber of Peers

Secretary-Archivist of the Chamber of Peers

Defender of the Marshal

A Vicomte

A Baron

An Officer

An Usher

An officer of Veterans

A Veteran

Peers of France

Superior Officer

The Marechale

1st Child of Marshal Ney

2nd Child of Marshal Ney

Solicitors, Ladies, Police, Veterans, Citizens, People.

SCENE I

An Antechamber. An entrance door. A door to the King's Office. Table, chairs, benches.

AT RISE, solicitors are seated or walking about.

USHER (emerging from the King's Office)

Everybody can withdraw—His Majesty won't receive more today, except great entrances.

(the solicitors leave with annoyance)

BARON

His Majesty doubtless wishes to remain alone to deal with great interests of state.

USHER

His Majesty just sat down to eat.

VICOMTE (who's just entered)

It's true, my dear Baron—he deigns to eat at this

moment. I had the luck to see him and surprise the arrival of a superb goose, an august smile of which I was able to seize at least half for myself.

BARON

How lucky you are to have been received! No doubt you know something.

VICOMTE

The mind of the King is very nice for the rest of us Peers of the Realm, the rest of you, too, brave deputies of the legal side—and to the entire immigration.

BARON

It's coming at last, then?

VICOMTE

It's a question of the law of indemnity.

BARON

We will get it.

VICOMTE

Yes, but not yet.

BARON

Perhaps they fear The Chamber of Peers.

VICOMTE

The Chamber of Peers will refuse nothing—but the pepper isn't ripe yet. That's the opinion of the Duke of Wellington.

BARON

You've seen this dear Duke?

VICOMTE

He's lunching with the King, and His Majesty said to him in front of me: "My Dear Duke, after God, it's to you that I owe my throne, and I beg you to accept the baton of a Marshal of France."

BARON

What delicacy! Only a Bourbon is capable of such things.

VICOMTE

On the subject of Marshals of France—what's going on with the trial of Marshal Ney?

BARON

Why, the Permanent Council of War of the first military district must pronounce shortly on the question of competence.

VICOMTE

They should stop such puerilities once they know the will of the King.

BELLART (to the Duke de Richelieu as they enter)

I tell you, Milord Duke, that the choice of judges in the Council of War is very bad.

RICHELIEU

But, my dear Bellart, it's still necessary to use Army officers.

BELLART

Bah! They are almost all old comrades of the accused. Hold on, I call on these gentlemen. When one wants justice to triumph, one must first of all be sure of one's judges.

VICOMTE

Certainly, certainly.

BELLART

You will see what they will do. Luckily, I've foreseen everything, and the plan we are going to present to the King won't allow any means of subterfuge to the guilty.

RICHELIEU (to an usher)

My friend, announce us to His Majesty.

USHER

Milord Duke knows he can enter instantly as First Minister—but etiquette proscribes a delay of twenty minutes to the Procurer-General.

BELLART

But in the case of urgency—

RICHELIEU

All the same, my dear chap, custom opposes it.

BARON

Etiquette above all.

VICOMTE

No doubt, no doubt—we mustn't lose good doctrines.

No concessions to the Revolution.

(The Usher enters the King's office)

If the Procurer-General would like the White-Flag to distract him—

(offering a newspaper)

BELLART

Excellent newspaper—I esteem the wit, and especially the character of its editor in-chief. His duel with Pecq did him much honor.

GENERAL (entering)

The Usher of the Office?

(looking for him)

BELLART (aside)

He's a general of the Empire. Let's be reserved.

GENERAL

I don't see him— Gentlemen, could you tell me if it's possible to reach the King?

BELLART

Sire, we are waiting—us— Thus a person foreign to the court—

GENERAL

I confess that I am not a courtier, and I indeed keep from fighting for that title— But the message I am charged to deliver to the King is important, and I desire to deliver it myself—to judge with my own eyes the impression that this news will produce on His Majesty.

RICHELIEU

Impossible, sir.

VICOMTE

Impossible, impossible.

(The Usher appears)

GENERAL

Still, if someone could say to His Majesty that it's a question of a great trial!

BELLART

And do you know something—?

GENERAL

The discussion lasted much less long than anticipated.

RICHELIEU

Then it's over?

GENERAL

Yes, gentlemen.

BELLART

And the judges have decided —?

GENERAL

The Council of War—composed of Marshals Jourdan, Masseus, Augeraux, Generals Gazan, Villate, and Claparede, declared themselves incompetent by a majority of five to two.

BELLART

I actually told you there were only two good ones.

RICHELIEU

It's treason.

BARON

Infamy.

VICOMTE

A denial of justice.

BELLART

I will prove it's a conspiracy.

GENERAL

Sir, I won't suffer that in front of me brave soldiers are slandered—my old companions-in-arms. They voted according to their conscience, and I desire that all the organs of justice not consult anything except the voice of their heart—which leaves after it neither remorse nor regret.

BELLART

Sir, I beg you to observe that you are speaking before the Council President.

GENERAL

Milord de Richelieu—Ah, I bless heaven—Milord Duke— They generally concede you are of a humane and gracious character; well, if it's true that I myself cannot get to the King, would you kindly bring him news of this preliminary decision so favorable to the accused, the opinion of these old soldiers, honored even by their enemies—which will perhaps inspire His Majesty with a decision worthy of him—Ney without doubt will be set at liberty, and it's to you that he will owe it—Milord Duke, it's a friend, a brother-in-arms of the bravest of the brave who begs you not to reject his demand.

RICHELIEU

General, I excuse the zeal that makes you act, but it cannot extend to the point of dictating rules of conduct to the Prime Minister of the King of France.

GENERAL

And you, sir?

BELLART

I am the prosecutor in the courts of justice, and I cannot constitute myself defender of a crime.

GENERAL

A crime. But the Council of War didn't treat the Marshal as a criminal.

BELLART

The triumph of faction will be of short duration,

because it's not only in the name of the King, in the name of France, but in the name of all Europe, that we are demanding a dazzling reparation.

VICOMTE (low to Baron)

Certainly, it will please the Holy Alliance.

USHER

Milord Duke and the Procurer-General can see His Majesty.

BELLART (to General)

Sir, the King will know the truth and you will soon know his response.

(He leaves with the Duke)

BARON (to General)

Trust me, General, don't be obstinate in trying to see the King.

(he leaves)

GENERAL

All against him.

VICOMTE

Ah, damn—we are no longer under the scepter of the usurper.

(he leaves)

GENERAL

No—we are no longer under the reign of the Emperor. I notice Madame Hatzfeld was luckier than the spouse of our unfortunate Labedoyere— What are they going to do with Marshal Ney now? Perhaps bring him before a Provost Court? Ah, they are capable of anything. This Bellart spoke of Europe—could it be that the Foreign Ambassadors?—oh, no—I cannot believe it.

WELLINGTON (emerging from the King's office—to Usher)

My friend, be so kind as to inform my people—

GENERAL

Lord Wellington! He knows me. Let's not let this opportunity escape.

WELLINGTON

What! You here, general? I thought that you didn't come to the court.

GENERAL

When I came here, France had not been invaded by foreigners.

WELLINGTON

Still proud!

GENERAL

I haven't lost the right to be; but if you still honor me with some esteem, be pleased, milord, to reply to a question which interests the honor of the Allied Sovereigns.

WELLINGTON

What's that?

GENERAL

Is it true that the Ambassadors of the Three Powers think that the security of Europe demands the condemnation of the unfortunate Marshal Ney?

WELLINGTON

Marshal Ney again.

GENERAL (repressing a reaction)

Milord Duke, I beg you to reply.

WELLINGTON

But I assure you that your opposition goes very far in their conjectures— I don't believe that such advice has ever been expressed by diplomacy.

GENERAL

Well, in that case, the Law of Nations places Marshal Ney under the safeguard of the Treaty of July 3rd— because the Capitulation of Paris states that no one can be disturbed nor investigated for his conduct or his political opinions.

WELLINGTON

It says that?

GENERAL

I signed it, and you, too, Milord.

WELLINGTON

General, I despair being unable to lend you my support, but the convention of July 3rd was never ratified by the King of France.

GENERAL

It was your duty to force him to do so—because it was only on this condition that we surrendered Paris. Without the confidence that we had in the faith of treaties, we would have enshrouded ourselves in the ruin of the Capital, rather than abandon our brave brothers-in-arms to the ax of the executioners of the Restoration.

WELLINGTON

What do you want? It's unfortunate, very unfortunate, but this oversight, this vice of form, separates us from the power to meddle in anything in the acts of government of Louis XVIII— But pardon, they're expecting me in your Naval Ministry. France is building much— much too much—and your King has just authorized me to complain about it.

(he bows and leaves)

GENERAL

Poor France—a shipwreck so beautiful and glorious— now, so humiliated. Ah, something says to me, "One day she'll arise more glorious and more beautiful—"

But my friend, my unfortunate friend— Ah, the Procurer of the King.

BELLART

You waited for us, sir—so much the better.

GENERAL

What new measure has been decreed?

RICHELIEU

General, we could only afflict you— It would be better that you learn from others.

GENERAL

I beg you—make my unease cease.

BELLART

Since you wish it—I'm going to give you knowledge of the principal articles of a new decree of His Majesty.

(reading)

"The Chamber of Peers will proceed without delay in the trial of Marshal Ney accused of High Treason."

GENERAL (aside)

The Chamber of Peers.

BELLART (reading)

"The present order will be delivered to the Chamber by our ministers, secretaries of state, and our Procurer-General near our royal court in Paris—"

GENERAL (aside)

Him!

BELLART (reading)

"That we charge to sustain the accusation and discussion. Given at our Château of the Tuilleries the 11th day of November of the year 1815—and of our reign, the 18th."

(speaking)

I told you so, sir—that the reply of the King would not be slow in coming.

CHAMBERLAIN

The King!

SEVERAL VOICES

The King! The King!

GENERAL

The King! If I could see him, speak to him for a moment.

RICHELIEU

Request an audience—but today it's impossible.

BELLART

His Majesty is going to mount his carriage to take a ride as far as Saint Ouen.

RICHELIEU

Are you coming, Bellart?

BELLART

To the Chamber of Peers.

GENERAL (to himself)

The Chamber of Peers! Bellart! He's lost.

USHER

The King!

(The Court can be seen passing at the back. The curtain falls.)

CURTAIN

SCENE II

The Chamber of Peers. The Chamber is set up as a council-hall. Several commissioners of the king are on benches.

BELLART

The Peers are really slow deciding. The delay of an hour that they granted to the Defense is about to expire. I'd really like to get this over with.

(Lanjuinais and the General arrive in a state of visible agitation)

LANJUINAIS (with rage)

It's not possible to reason with them. You'd say it's decided in advance.

GENERAL

What's happening?

LANJUINAIS

You weren't in the Council Chamber, General?

GENERAL

No—I thought that the suspension of the hearing had only one purpose—to give some rest to the defenders—could they have deliberated?

LANJUINAIS

At this very moment they are deciding if the Marshal will be permitted to invoke the Capitulation.

GENERAL

That's his right.

LANJUINAIS

I thought like you; I raised my voice in his favor—but, I really fear— Hold on, my dear friend, I tell you with sorrow—they will do whatever so that their condemnation will have the air of partisan vengeance. It seems that each witness against the poor Marshal obeys a foreign impulse. Until the turncoat of Waterloo speaks of fidelity, what a sorrowful spectacle this trial is! Posterity won't believe it.

GENERAL

And these dishonest sovereigns who with a single word could snatch him from death. They'll allow him to be shot.

LANJUINAIS

They will never pardon him his glory. It's the French Army they want to strike, in its most illustrious general. The bullet which strikes him is addressed to the heart of the nation.

GENERAL (perceiving Bellart)

Look at the hangdog face of the Public Accuser. That man makes me shiver.

LANJUINAIS

He reminds me of Fouquier-Thinville. You'd think you are looking at a bird of prey.

GENERAL

It's true. There are bullies who have the misfortune to resemble him.

LANJUINAIS

But no question, the deliberations are over. I notice one of our colleagues.

VICOMTE (entering like a man in a hurry)

Usher, I beg you to inform my coachman to to bring around my carriage.

GENERAL

Are you leaving, Vicomte?

VICOMTE

Yes, yes, my dear boy, all these skirmishes do me up—I've got a headache, and then I'm dining with Wellington.

LANJUINAIS (ironic)

Ah—with Wellington.

VICOMTE

You conceive it wouldn't be polite to miss such an honorable invitation—but I'll return for the sentencing.

(All the Peers reenter, one by one. The President takes his seat.)

PRESIDENT

Usher—make the accused come in.

(Pause. The Marshal enters.)

The hearing resumes. Gentlemen defenders resume.

BARON (low to another peer near him)

No question we will pronounce the sentence this evening.

DEFENDER (rising)

I believe to have, in the first part of the defense, completely finished. Marshal Ney, regarding premeditation in the crime of which he is accused. I think to have demonstrated to the last iota of evidence that the Marshal foresaw nothing, meditated nothing.

(reaction)

In all his conduct, in all his actions, he had no other end in view than the fatherland, it was constantly the object of his sacred cult. Yet another point, it must be attributed exclusively to the Marshal the ardent desire he had to avoid some Frenchmen shedding the blood of other Frenchmen.

(reaction)

Moreover, gentlemen, a political transaction militates in favor of the Marshal—the Treaty of July 3rd.

BELLART

I formally object to that being invoked by the defense.

DEFENDER

Because it would serve the accused.

BELLART

Because it is null in the eyes of the King.

DEFENDER

It's worthy of the eyes of France.

BELLART (to President)

It's time to make such scandals cease.

PRESIDENT

In virtue of the discretionary power invested in me, I would have to object to the Defenders developing the foreign means which they would invoke—nonetheless, I have consulted the Chamber on this point—and a large majority is of my opinion. I forbid the defenders from arguing on the basis of a treaty which the King is not party to, of a treaty which is more than foreign to His Majesty, since twenty-one days later, in the very presence of sovereign allies, he rendered his decree of July 24th which annulled it. I direct the defenders not to employ arguments which have no connection to the facts of the accusation.

DEFENDER

We have great respect for decisions of the Court to allow ourselves any comments on the ruling it has just issued. The observation that I want to make now is directed to a later treaty, that of 20 November, which can surely be invoked. Sarrelouis, where the Marshal was born, is no longer part of France.

(reaction by the Marshal)

Thus—

NEY (rising and addressing his attorney)

Sir! Sir! I don't want to save myself through a cowardly act! I am French! I will die French!

(turning to Peers)

Up to this point, my defense seemed free. I perceive that it is shackled. I thank my generous defenders for what they have done and for what they are ready to do—but I prefer not to be defended at all then to have only a sham defense. I am accused contra the faith of treaties, and they don't want me to invoke them. Well—I call on Europe and posterity.

BELLART

They've pushed the liberty of defense to the point of license and dare to complain.

(murmurings)

The Commissioners of the King who made these decisions of the Marshal refer to what has just been said. Mr. President, resume the hearing.

NEY

And as for me, I protest with all the strength of my indignation against this denial of justice.

PRESIDENT (to defenders)

Continue the defense and confine yourselves to the facts.

NEY (to his defenders)

I enjoin you not to speak unless they permit you to defend me freely.

PRESIDENT

Accused, you are compromising your case.

MARECHALE

And you, your honor, Mr. President.

PRESIDENT

Address yourself to the court with respect!

NEY

In that case, don't judge me without listening to me.

BELLART

Since the Marshal wants to conclude the struggle, we won't make new observations on our side, and will end with our requests. The Commissioners of the King request that it please the Court to declare Marshal Ney, Marshal of France, Duke de Elchingen, Prince of Moscow, guilty of having culpable understanding with Bonaparte, giving intelligence that had the effect of facilitating him and his gang.

NEY (interrupting him with indignation)

His gang! There are then no old soldiers here.

PRESIDENT

Marshal, you must not interrupt.

BELLART (continuing)

For having gone over to the enemy with a party of troops, finally for having committed treason to the King and the State, by taking part in a conspiracy whose end was to dishonor the government and the order of succsssion to the throne. In consequence, The Commissioners of The King request that Marshal Ney be condemned to capital punishment.

PRESIDENT

Accused, do you have something to say?

NEY

A last word. You judge me when everything is over. You do not take into account the terrible circumstances in which I found myself, because, as I've told you, the 14th was no longer time to think of resistance. Bonaparte was advancing with giant steps; the population pressed around him and greeted him with unanimous exclamations. They kissed the eagle with distraction or saluted, weeping, the Flag of the the Republic or Empire. If I betrayed, all France had betrayed before me.

PRESIDENT

Make the accused withdraw along with the witnesses and the general public.

(The Marshal leaves with the defenders, witnesses and the audience.)

PRESIDENT

I'm going to pose the first question. Did Marshal Ney receive emissaries on the 13th and 14th of March? Proceed to the roll call.

(The peers head towards the urns and deposit their votes. They call successively in a loud voice the following peers.)

The Duke of Uze

The Marquis of Breze

The Marquis de Guiche

The Marquis d'Avaray.

The Count de Lanjuinais.

LANJUINAIS (from his seat)

Article 12 of the of the Convention of Paris applies to the accused or a person. They refused him the benefit of it. We, the Count de Lauguinais, Count de Nicolai, Marquis d'Aligre, Duke de Broglie declare that we won't vote an assassination.[1]

(Agitation, the roll call continues)

The Count de Semonville.

CURTAIN

---

1. The Duke de Broglie voted no to all questions.

SCENE III

The Luxembourg. Inside Ney's prison cell. A bed. Ney is seated with two defenders.

A moment of silence at first.

DEFENDER

I repeat to you, Marshal—such a long deliberation is a good omen. You have devoted friends in the noble court.

NEY

Not many.

DEFENDER

Your brothers-in-arms.

NEY

My brothers-in-arms? Yes, maybe. Grenier, Klein, Gouvion—those will remember the unlucky Ney—the others—

(with a bitter smile)

They mustn't compromise themselves.

DEFENDER

That would be a cowardly act that history would wither.

NEY

My God, gentlemen, at the moment you are cradling hopes—the decision has been rendered—no question.

DEFENDER

We will be called to hear it; they will come to inform us.

OFFICER OF THE ROYAL GRENADIERS (entering)

Gentlemen Defenders, the Chamber of Peers demands that you appear and be present at the reading of the judgement.

(The Defenders shiver. Ney remains calm.)

NEY (after a moment of silence)

Go.

DEFENDER

We shall return.

NEY

Yes, I will say goodbye to you.

(he shakes their hands with affection)

Goodbye—and forever! They have some hope. At least they tell me so. That's their affair. Until the fatal blindfold is placed over the eyes of the condemned they say to him: hope—and such is human weakness that we need to believe them.

(vehemently)

Where will this rage to kill that animates them stop? When will the list of victims end? We haven't shed enough blood on the fields of battle—we must shed the last drops on the scaffold. Poor Labedoyere, you indeed judged these folks.

(pulls from his breast a letter that he slowly unfolds.)

I'm the one who received your last confidence. You foresaw my fate. This letter makes me ill and I keep rereading it.

(reads and stops at almost every word)

"They've come to get me. My executioners are here. Ten more minutes and my patriotic heart will have ceased to beat. I'm asking for pen and ink. I'm writing you. Flee, Marshal! In France, now, they don't pardon glory. They are going to assassinate me."

(weeping)

Brave young man! You thought of your old general as you died.

(he puts his hand over his eyes, and strides about—after a pause)

I'm tired—these long arguments, these torturing questions. I feel some hours of sleep would do me good.

(he casts himself on his bed)

Perhaps they may not come until tomorrow.

(he sleeps by degrees)

And down there, at Saint Helena, at this very moment, perhaps, you are thinking of me—of the one you called the bravest of the brave. Napoleon! Napoleon!

(He repeats the same phrase again and falls asleep. At this moment the noise of the key opening the door to the Marshal's cell can be heard)

OFFICER (entering)

He's sleeping—Milord Marshal!

NEY (rising with a start)

What do you want with me?

(noticing the secretary)

Ah, it's you, Mr. Secretary—already.

SECRETARY

I'm in despair to have awakened The Marshal.

NEY

That's nothing. I'll resume my sleeping later. You are bringing me the decree of the noble court.

(The Secretary makes an affirmative sign)

I am ready to hear you, read—

SECRETARY

Seen by the Chamber, the act of accusation drawn up on the 16th of November by the Commissioners of the King, named by the decree of His Majesty, the 11th and the 13th of the aforesaid month, against Marshal Ney, Marshal of France, Duke of Elchingen—

NEY (interrupting him)

Say Marshal Ney and a bit of dust—

SECRETARY

Seen by the decree taken of seizing the body, the 17th aforesaid of the month of November, against the aforesaid Marshal Ney. Heard the witnesses cited at the request of the Public Ministry, the witnesses cited by the accused, the ministry public had the conclusions.

And the defenders of the accused in their pleadings.

The Chamber after having deliberated, awaited the result of the indictment and debates— That Marshal Ney is convicted of having—during the night of the 13th and 14th of March 1815—greeted emissaries of the usurper, of having immediately given the order to his troops to join Bonaparte, and having himself, at their head, brought about this reunion.

Declares him guilty of crimes under Articles 77, 87, 88, and 102 of the Penal Code. Consequently, applying the aforesaid articles—

Condemns Michel Ney, Marshal of France, Duke of Elchingen, Prince of Moscow, Ex-Peer of France, to the pain of death.

Orders that the execution shall take place at the diligence of the Commissioners of the King.

(The voice of the Secretary is moved. The two Royal Grenadiersare in tears The Marshal is impassive.)

NEY

That's fine: you can withdraw.

SECRETARY

That's not all.

NEY

What more?

SECRETARY

After the judgment the Procurer-General has requested and the President has pronounced that the law of 24 Ventose, year XII—that the condemned be degraded from the Legion of Honor.

NEY (in a terrible voice)

Degraded!

(after a pause)

That's fine.

(tears off his decorations)

Take these to the King of France and thank him on my behalf.

SECRETARY

If you wish to see Madame Marechale and your children—

NEY

Oh—yes, sir, yes, I desire it quite excitedly.

SECRETARY

They are here.

NEY

I hope you haven't been barbarous enough to tell them I am comdemned.

SECRETARY

Ah, Milord Marshal.

NEY (shaking his hand)

Pardon. Make them come in.

(The Secretary leaves.)

My wife—my children—courage—it's necessary.

(The Marechale and her two children, Madame Gamot, the sister-in-law of the Marshal enter. The Marechale rushes to the arms of her husband, but falls violently on the floor.)

NEY (running to her)

My friends, help me to succor her.

CHILDREN (leaning over their mother)

Mother! Mother!

NEY (exasperated)

They've killed her.

ROYAL GRENADIER

Poor woman. That makes me weep.

MADAME GAMOT

Silence! She's opening her eyes.

MARECHALE (raising her head with effort, placing her hand in front of her face.)

Where am I? Who's brought me here?

(looking around her, seeing Ney)

Ah!

(she runs to his arms)

It's him! It's him! I won't leave him anymore.

NEY

Come to yourself. We still have hope remaining.

MARECHALE

None. I know everything.

NEY

They deceived you.

MARECHALE

Oh, no.

NEY

Speak lower at least. Our children will hear you.

MARECHALE

Cruel people! They wouldn't listen to me! Still, I besieged their door. I dragged myself on my knees shouting to them—

Mercy! Mercy!

NEY

I don't want that.

MARECHALE

Oh—it's that it goes to the happiness of my entire life. Nothing will remain to me if I lose you. Prayers, supplications—it's all been useless. They are not men, they are tigers.

NEY

Calm down, calm down. Don't poison the sweetness of our last moments. Your despair will dissipate the happy ignorance of our children. Your shouts will warn them of my danger. And I won't be able to press them in my arms. Don't take them from my arms, I have to say goodbye to them, too. Don't take from me the strength that I need for this cruel and sweet moment.

MARECHALE (with effort)

Yes, I'll shut up. I will impose silence on my sorrow.

NEY (gently)

We will leave each other on this earth, but we will see each other again on high.

(they bring the children closer)

ONE OF THE BOYS

Father, my aunt told me that you were going to leave this villainous room. You will come with us, right?

NEY

Yes, my children.

CHILD

Soon?

NEY

Soon!

(he sits down then presses them to his heart)

I'm leaving here, kids—to go—anyway—somewhere I'll be better. I will be separated for some time. Your mother will remain with you. Be worthy of the cares she will lavish on you. Love her well. Love her as you love me. Love France, too. Because France is your second mother. When you grow up, if a heart beats in your breast remember that you bear a glorious name, yes, glorious. They will tell you about my life. Let it serve you as an example. Because it is pure—and if your country calls you to defend it and be more lucky than your father—try to die on the field of battle.

(The door opens and the clerk and several officers of

the Royal Grenadiers appear.)

(The weeping Marechale runs toward the Marshal, who stops, clasps her a last time to his heart then rushes with a firm step, making an imperative gesture to the officers.)

MARECHALE (letting out a scream)

My God! They are here.

NEY (running to her)

Yet another sacrifice to our children.

(The Marechale hurls herself into the arms of her sister-in-law, bawling)

It's over.

(He casts a last look at this children, dries a tear and says to officers)

I am ready. Let's march.

(FREEZE FRAME: The weeping Marechale runs towards the Marshal, who stops, clasps her to his heart, then rushes with a firm step, making an imperative gesture to the officers.)

CURTAIN

SCENE IV

A place near the Observatory.

AN OFFICER OF THE POLICE

It's here, gentlemen, place yourselves there—you will watch the public—mainly the veterans charged with the execution. Be very careful that no one suspect you are police.

(A squad of uniformed gendarmes arrives. The officer makes them form a cordon.)

Gendarmes think that you are here to protect justice; the people don't love you, but the government loves us, and the proof is there will be a distribution when you return to quarters. Long live the King!

GENERAL (enters, wrapped in a cloak, aside)

Lots of people already; they didn't deceive me—this is the fateful place. What weather! How sad and dark! It's ten years almost to the very day it was the sun of Austerlitz.

(comes forward)

OFFICER

You cannot pass, sir.

GENERAL

Why?

OFFICER

Orders. Besides, what are you coming here to do?

GENERAL (pointing to the populace)

I'm coming here, like all these brave folk, for a last, a sorrowful goodbye.

OFFICER

It's not here—it's at the plain of Grenelle.

GENERAL (to people)

Don't believe a word of it. That rumor's being spread to deceive the friends of the Marshal. And to carry away a last consolation to his misfortune.

OFFICER

Then—get back and remain if you wish. But you won't

see him, because they've just assured me that the King has pardoned him.

GENERAL

That's a new imposture. Pardon—no, my friends, no. They are thirsty for his blood a second time; the Marechale rushed before the carriage of the King imploring his clemency—they pushed her back without pity, and the unfortunate thought to be trampled under the feet of the horses.

OFFICER

Sir, cease to express these seditious remarks or I'll place you under arrest.

GENERAL (opening his cloak)

Dare lay a hand on a Marshal of France!

OFFICER (aside)

A Marshal! No scandal. I will denounce him.

(shouting)

The Carriage! The Carriage! Here he is! Here he is!

GENERAL (to himself)

His last hour has rung. Yes, here he is. What recognition! What courage! Oh, I cannot hold back my tears.

OFFICER AND POLICE

Get back! Get back!

(They form a line to retain the curious and the spectators.)

(Veterans arrange themselves facing a small wall. The gendarmes in curves are behind them. Ney is dressed in a blue overcoat, short pants, black silk stockings, buckled shoes, round hat—he enters slowly and bows to all sides with dignity.)

GENERAL

He saw me!

(running to him)

Ney, my friend!

NEY

You here, my old comrade.

(A superior officer prevents the officer and guardsmen from separating them)

GENERAL

Weren't we together on our first battlefield?

NEY

I heard you. I must await you here.

GENERAL (low)

I'm armed. Say the word, I will make a desperate attempt.

NEY

Watch yourself. Don't give your head to these folks. One's enough for today.

(confused shouting)

GENERAL

What's that uproar?

(looking)

An order—if only it were a reprieve.

(a gendarme arrives and delivers a letter to the officer of the gendarmes. Everyone looks on with anxiety.)

OFFICER OF GENDARMES (after glancing at the letter)

Everyone get back.

GENERAL

All is lost.

(He casts himself in the arms of the Marshal)

OFFICER (to his superior officer)

The letter advises me that the populace is undeceived and running en masse through the boulevards.

(the shouting gets closer)

OFFICER

You hear? We must get this over with.

NEY

Goodbye, general. Speak often of me to my children.

(He bows again to the people. The Officer in charge offers him a white blindfold.)

Are you unaware, sir, that for the last twenty-five years I've been accustomed to face bullets and cannon balls?

(placing himself facing the veterans)

I protest before God and men the iniquity of my sentence. Long live France.

(he tosses his hat a few feet away)

Soldier, get ready, prepare your weapons.

(The soldiers remain motionless; the shouting off increases and gets claoser)

You hesitate—do your duty.

(taking a step—hand on his heart)

Hurry and aim— Aim! Fire!

(The Veterans shoot, The Marshal falls—and shortly after the detonation people arrive in great numbers. They break through the line of gendarmes and the body is found covered.)

GENERAL (to Veterans who are all downcast)

You've just killed the most intrepid of your generals.

VETERAN

At least it wasn't me.

(He fires his rifle in the air)

(Meanwhile, the Marshal's body is placed on a stretcher and soldiers carry it away.)

GENERAL

Stop a moment, a single moment, so that I can see his inanimate remains one last time.

(He places one hand on the cadaver and kneels on the ground)

Goodbye, my friend, my brother-in-arms—your death will not efface your life.

History will say you were the bravest of the brave. It will say that your courage in Russia saved the remnants of the Grand Army—perhaps the sons of your judges. Goodbye, hero of Moscow. Brune and Labedoyère await your great shade on high, and posterity will reserve you a place in the Pantheon beside Montebello.

(rising)

And now, gentlemen, let pass the justice of the Chamber of Peers.

CURTAIN

ABOUT THE EDITOR

Frank J. Morlock has written and translated many plays since retiring from the legal profession in 1992. His translations have also appeared on Project Gutenberg, the Alexandre Dumas Père web page, Literature in the Age of Napoléon, Infinite Artistries. com, and Munsey's (formerly Blackmask). In 2006 he received an award from the North American Jules Verne Society for his translations of Verne's plays. He lives and works in México.

www.ingramcontent.com/pod-product-compliance
Lightning Source LLC
LaVergne TN
LVHW041620070426
835507LV00008B/357

Breaking Down Strongholds

McDougal & Associates

Servants of Christ and Stewards of the Mysteries of God

Breaking Down Strongholds

by

Desmond Thomas

Unless otherwise noted, all scripture quotations are from the Authorized King James Version of the Bible. References marked "AMP" are from *The Amplified Bible*, copyright © 1954, 1958, 1962, 1964, 1965, 1987 by The Lockman Foundation, La Habra, California. Unless otherwise noted, all scripture word definitions are from *Strong's Exhaustive Concordance* of the Bible, Dugan Publishers, Inc., Gordonsville, Tennessee.

Breaking Down Strongholds
Copyright © 2015 — by Desmond A. S. Thomas
ALL RIGHTS RESERVED

All rights reserved under U.S. and international copyright conventions. Contents and/or cover may not be reproduced in whole or in part in any form without the express written consent of the publisher. No part of this book may be reproduced or transmitted in any form or by any means, electronic or mechanical, including photocopying, recording or by any information retrieval system.

Cover Design by Paulo Sergio Silva

Published by:

McDougal & Associates
18896 Greenwell Springs RD
Greenwell Springs, LA 70739
www.thepublishedword.com

McDougal & Associates is an organization dedicated to the spreading of the Gospel of Jesus Christ to as many people as possible in the shortest time possible.

ISBN 978-0-9543083-3-9

Printed in the US, the UK and Australia
For Worldwide Distribution

When a strong man armed keepeth his palace, his goods are in peace: But when a stronger than he shall come upon him, and overcome him, he taketh from him all his armour wherein he trusted, and divideth his spoils.   Luke 11:21

Say: "I AM STRONGER THAN HE!"

(For the weapons of our warfare are not carnal, but mighty through God to the pulling down of strong holds;) casting down imaginations, and every high thing that exalteth itself against the knowledge of God, and bringing into captivity every thought to the obedience of Christ; and having in a readiness to revenge all disobedience, when your obedience is fulfilled.
      2 Corinthians 10:4-6

Say: "I AM READY!"

DEDICATION

- To those who are silently suffering under demonic strongholds
- To those who try to explain to others what they are going through, only to be told that it is all in their minds
- To those who are fighting what they know not and don't understand, the mystery behind their misery

This book is dedicated to you. I hope you find in it some answers to your struggles.

CONTENTS

Foreword by Bishop Ed Nelson 9

Introduction 11
1. Destroying Evil Foundations 19
2. Appropriating Biblical Covenants 27
3. Destroying Demonic Strongholds 57
4. You Cannot Serve Two Masters 67
5. Destroying Religious Strongholds 79
6. Destroying Spiritual Prostitution 87
7. Destroying Territorial and Cultural Strongholds 95
8. Destroying Mental Strongholds 101
9. Identifying the Spiritual Strongman 113
10. Destroying Negative Altars 119
11. Destroying Negative Covenants and Dedications . 131
12. Defeating the Powers in the Heavenlies 141
13. Defeating Water Spirits 155
14. Destroying Hauntings 161
15. Prayers for Deliverance 167
16. Knowing Your Redemption 177
17. Conclusion 187

Ministry Page 193

Over many years now, I have known Desmond Thomas to carry a deep compassion for those bound in darkness and sin and a powerful gift from God to release them. He brings particular insight into African occult practice, which will be new to most Western readers. It is my prayer that this book may open eyes, prepare hearts and be a true vehicle of release to many, in Jesus' name.

Dr. Trevor Saxby,
Senior Pastoral Team,
Jesus Fellowship,
Northampton, UK

I first knew Desmond Thomas so many years ago as a teenage student in the Bible training center I was invited to establish with Pastor Ade Jones in Freetown, Sierra Leone. Since then, Desmond has come a long way. Freetown and Sierra Leone can be proud of their native son who has blessed the world with his burden to see men and women everywhere freed from demon influence. I am proud to be his publisher.

Harold McDougal
Greenwell Springs, Louisiana

FOREWORD BY BISHOP ED NELSON

For more than twenty-five years I have been actively involved in healing and deliverance ministry, and about twenty or more of those years I have known Pastor Desmond Thomas as an authority on this subject. I have witnessed his consistency and his willingness and love for the deliverance ministry. He has a great passion to break down demonic strongholds and bring God's people out of bondage.

In this book, *Breaking Down Strongholds*, the author lets us know how easily a person can be held in demonic strongholds and not even know it, and also how to get out and avoid demonic strongholds altogether. He achieves this by teaching us some of the cunningness, trickery and methodology of Satan's operation against us. This book will serve as an eye-opener for those Christians who are still ignorant of the devil's devices and demonic attacks on Christians, such as setbacks, financial insufficiencies, constant failures, suicidal thoughts, nervousness, drug and alcohol addictions, broken homes, marriage and success delays and even sickness and mental disorders.

As I mentioned in my own book, *Deliverance Is God's Design*, for many years our mental institutions and hospitals have been treating people who actually are struggling with spiritual attacks that led to their sickness or mental difficulties. No wonder their treatment has not been successful! Those who are ignorant of the possible spiritual causes behind a given ailment may not know that the Bible has numerous examples to prove that a person's illness or disposition may have its root in spiritual matters.

As a man's soul influences his body, likewise satanic forces can influence his soul, either through sickness or by inflicting misery on the man. In the pages of this book *Breaking Down Strongholds*, the author takes a close look at various scriptures validating his findings, thus providing guidance from the Word of God and also his own experience in the field of breaking down spiritual strongholds.

If Christians are to stay free from demonic strongholds, wisdom will suggest that the schemes of the enemy must be learned, and that can be accomplished by reading this book. The purpose of the book, then, is to let reverberate the scriptural words:

My people are destroyed for lack of knowledge. Hosea 4:6

Lest Satan should get an advantage of us: for we are not ignorant of his devices. 2 Corinthians 2:11

Satan and his co-hosts can make themselves appear as angels of light, but they are disruptive and destructive (see 2 Corinthians 11:14).

Bishop Ed Nelson Isibor
Fold of Christ Ministry
London, England

INTRODUCTION

Before you were born into this life, all of your sins were paid for by means of Jesus' death on the cross. All of your sicknesses were paid for, all of your poverty was paid for, and all your deliverance was paid for. That includes deliverance from every power of darkness. At some point, through the foolishness of preaching, you came to realize that Jesus loved you and died for you and you appropriated by faith your salvation.

Now you are a child of God. Why, then, do you still sometimes suffer the effects of the dominion of sin, sickness and other curses? Why does this world and the dominion of the devil have any hold over you at all? Why? Perhaps because you have been ignorant of your dominion in Christ and have not appropriated your complete deliverance based on the fact that Jesus made you a new creature. The devil has been taking advantage of you because of your ignorance, or perhaps, some unbelief and/or disobedience.

All of the promises of redemption through Christ must be appropriated by faith. It is by faith that we are saved (see Ephesians 2:8). As the apostle Paul declared to the Roman believers, *"The just shall live by faith"* (Romans 1:17).

But each aspect of our redemption through Christ must be individually received and appropriated on the grounds of faith. We don't necessarily get healed of our sicknesses when we receive the forgiveness of sin. We must believe and receive our healing separately, and deliverance is a part of the healing ministry.

Demons don't just leave us because we are saved. In fact, they will intensify their warfare against us, especially if we are coming from a demonic background where covenants were made over our lives. So when we are born again, the battle has just begun.

This book will teach you about spiritual warfare. It will open your eyes to know who your true enemies are. It will help you to understand how they operate and what the weapons are that they use against you. It will teach you how to disarm the enemy, by using your own weapons of warfare.

As believers in Christ, we don't yet know everything. There are many things that still remain a mystery to us. Often, we don't know why certain things are not working right for us, even though we live holy lives. The reason is that the devil operates in the dark, mysteriously. That's why his kingdom is called the kingdom of darkness.

This is your spiritual warfare handbook. It will serve as a guide for you to understand the demonic personalities that are responsible for your case and how to fight them. Paul wrote:

> *Lest Satan should get an advantage of us: for we are not ignorant of his devices.*   2 Corinthians 2:11

INTRODUCTION

The devil will always try you. Even Jesus did not escape trials, so who are we to escape them? Jesus had to use spiritual weapons to fight against this enemy, and we must do the same. Satan left Jesus for a while, but then he came back, and that's what he will do with you too. He will always come back, but don't worry; our victory over him is certain. That, however, does not mean that we will not have to fight him.

Some say, "The devil is a defeated foe," and they don't do any spiritual warfare. Then, before they can think about what has happened, they find themselves being enslaved by some kind of nasty sinful habit, and everything around them begins to take a downturn.

This is like standing in the middle of a battlefield while the devil is throwing arrows at you, and you are saying, "I have been delivered," but you're not using your shield of faith or your Sword of the Spirit (which is the Word of God). He did not give you these weapons for nothing. You are to use them, and so you must know how to use them. This is precisely what this book is all about.

Many of those who find themselves in the mission fields of the world are trying to deliver people from the powers of darkness that bind them, but they cannot be effective against these forces because their ignorance about demons and how to deal with them limits them. This is your guide to spiritual warfare for effective evangelism. Read it with an open mind and with an open spirit, and receive from God, in Jesus' name. Amen!

Before this earth we live in was in its current condition, the Bible let's us know:

> *The earth was without form, and void; and darkness was upon the face of the deep.*   Genesis 1:2

> *For this they willingly are ignorant of, that by the word of God the heavens were of old, and the earth standing out of the water and in the water: whereby the world that then was, being overflowed with water, perished.*
> 2 Peter 3:5-6

What the problem was with the earth, we can't say, but we do know that it was destroyed. Then God had to recreate the earth, and the result was the new earth we now know:

> *But the heavens and the earth, which are now, by the same word are kept in store, reserved unto fire against the Day of Judgment and perdition of ungodly men.*
> 2 Peter 3:7

Sometime before or during the time of the first and second earth, there was war in Heaven. Lucifer, the anointed cherub, revolted against God with one third of Heaven's angels. Unfortunately for them, they lost the battle in their rebellion. Michael the Archangel defeated Lucifer with his one-third of the angels. They could no longer be tolerated in Heaven and were driven to the earth:

> *And there was war in heaven: Michael and his angels fought against the dragon; and the dragon fought and his angels, and prevailed not; neither was their place found*

INTRODUCTION

any more in heaven. And the great dragon was cast out, that old serpent, called the Devil, and Satan, which deceiveth the whole world: he was cast out into the earth, and his angels were cast out with him.

Revelation 12:7-9

So, you have now familiarized yourselves with rebel angels who have made their abode in the earth. The Scriptures also tell us of others who are now imprisoned under darkness:

And the angels, which kept not their first estate, but left their own habitation, he hath reserved in everlasting chains under darkness unto the judgment of the great day. Jude 1:6

Some teach that there are also creatures that survived the destruction of the first earth and made their way to this new earth and are a part of these alien entities. Since the Scriptures have nothing to say about them, we will leave that matter alone.

From the Scriptures we also understand that these rebel angels have set their kingdom in strategic places — the heavenlies, the high places of the earth and also in the seas and rivers and forests — and have built themselves strongholds in these places. These deceptive spirits seek to make contact with mankind with the intention to kill, steal and destroy the human race, all in retaliation against God, who made us in His own image and likeness. So there is a constant war going on with these spiritual beings:

For we wrestle not against flesh and blood, but against principalities, against powers, against the rulers of the darkness of this world, against spiritual wickedness in high places. Ephesians 6:12

In that day the LORD with his sore and great and strong sword shall punish leviathan the piercing serpent, even leviathan that crooked serpent; and he shall slay the dragon that is in the sea. Isaiah 27:1

Behold, I give unto you power to tread on serpents and scorpions, and over all the power of the enemy: and nothing shall by any means hurt you. Luke 10:19

My point here is not what you call these creatures — gods, demigods, demons, evil spirits, jinni or something else — but the fact that these negative supernatural strongholds exist.

After his fall, the first appearance of Lucifer, the head of this kingdom, was in the Garden of Eden where he was tempting Eve. He appeared in the form of a serpent talking to her. You cannot underestimate the ability of these spiritual beings to transform or take the form of animals, birds or even human beings, anything to make contact with people:

Now the serpent was subtler than any beast of the field which the LORD God had made. And he said unto the woman, Yea, hath God said, Ye shall not eat of every tree of the garden? Genesis 3:1

INTRODUCTION

Thou hast been in Eden the garden of God. ... Thou art the anointed cherub that covereth.   Ezekiel 28:13-14

In some cases, people try to make contact with these evil spirits and seek them for help. My purpose here is to explain what a point of contact with the negative supernatural is, how these points of contact are established and renewed and how they can be revoked and broken.

You also need to understand that God, the Father of Spirits, is the only One you are to seek and to give worship to. You are not to seek after any other god, angels (whether good or evil), demons, familiar spirits, spirits of the dead, spirits in the forest, river, sea or ancestral spirits. Seeking any of these is an error, and the end thereof will be highly detrimental to you and your family:

Let no man beguile you of your reward in a voluntary humility and worshipping of angels, intruding into those things which he hath not seen, vainly puffed up by his fleshly mind.   Colossians 2:18

Regard not them that have familiar spirits, neither seek after wizards, to be defiled by them: I am the LORD your God.   Leviticus 19:31

There shall not be found among you any one that maketh his son or his daughter to pass through the fire, or that useth divination, or an observer of times, or an enchanter, or a witch, or a charmer, or a consulter with familiar spirits, or a wizard, or a necromancer. For all that do these things are an abomination unto the LORD: and because of these abominations the LORD thy God doth drive them out from before thee. Deuteronomy 18:10-12

Some people have ignorantly consulted evil spirits, either by themselves or through a medium. Others have contracts with these spirits through the dedications of their parents or ancestors, something they never gave their consent to. This book will open your eyes to these things and show you how to be delivered from their influences. This book will offer deliverance to the captives and open your spiritual understanding to the truth of God's Word, in Jesus' name.

Get ready to enter the unknown. What you are about to read will open your eyes to the mystery behind your misery or the misery of someone you know. Read prayerfully and with an open heart, and the Lord will help you. May God bless you and open your spiritual eyes as you read, in Jesus' name. Amen!

Desmond Thomas
London, England

Chapter 1

DESTROYING EVIL FOUNDATIONS

And the LORD said unto Moses, Write this for a memorial in a book, and rehearse it in the ears of Joshua: for I will utterly put out the remembrance of Amalek from under heaven. And Moses built an altar, and called the name of it Jehovahnissi: for he said, Because the LORD hath sworn that the LORD will have war with Amalek from generation to generation. Exodus 17:14-16

After the children of Israel came out of Egypt, Amalek was the first of the pagan kings who summoned up the courage to fight them. Moses, Aaron and Hur went up to a mountain, and Moses lifted his hands up to Heaven, with the rod of God in his hand, while Joshua led the fight against Amalek. Whenever Moses' hands became weary, Amalek prevailed, so Hur and Aaron held his hands up until Amalek was defeated. From this warfare with Amalek we learn some interesting things.

The war with Amalek was won at the mountain. Israel prevailed only when Moses' hands were up, so his hands were kept lifted to God in persisting, prevailing prayers from morning till evening. This was a physical battle, but it was won spiritually, through prayer.

God promised to utterly blot out the memory of Amalek under Heaven. This meant that the fight with Amalek would cease because Amalek would be totally wiped out and removed from the memory of God's people. Because of this, Moses built an altar and called it Jehovah-Nissi meaning, "the Lord is my Banner." This reveals God as our Banner in warfare. His name, in spiritual warfare, is Jehovah-Nissi, and with His banner unfurled over us, we are assured of victory.

The New Covenant shows that it is Jesus who gives us victory:

> *But thanks be to God, which giveth us the victory through our Lord Jesus Christ.*   1 Corinthians 15:57

Lastly, Amalek also represent something generational. The struggle with Amalek was a generational struggle, a generational warfare.

AMALEK AND ANCESTRAL SINS

I consider Amalek to be an ancestral spirit. I also consider the battle with Amalek to be a battle against sin, as sin is also generational. Through Adam's transgression, we have all inherited sin, and we must all battle against it:

> *Wherefore, as by one man sin entered into the world, and death by sin; and so death passed upon all men, for that all have sinned.*   Romans 5:12

DESTROYING EVIL FOUNDATIONS

Abraham fought against lying. He lied about his wife being his sister, and we see Isaac also fighting the same battle and the very same lie (see Genesis 12:13 and 26:6-8). Today, there are those who hate the way their father or mother lived, and they try to fight their way through, so as not to live the same way, but they often end up living just like their parents did. Men often become alcoholics, like their fathers before them, or they sire children from various women and don't take care of those children, just like their fathers did. They repeat the sins of their fathers.

These are ancestral sins. Some children not only take the names of their parents; they also repeat their parents' sins, carry their sicknesses and suffer the same scandals. The reason for this is that the same ancestral spirit who was in their father has now re-emerged in them, yielding the same fruits as in their forefathers. They fight with Amalek from generation to generation, and Amalek has become a stronghold in their family line.

As a believer, you are not under a curse (including ancestral curses), but you may have to fight against the evil effects of those curses in your family line. By faith, you can appropriate your deliverance from the effects of those curses by means of Jesus' death on a tree for our redemption from every curse:

> *Christ hath redeemed us from the curse of the law, being made a curse for us: for it is written, Cursed is every one that hangeth on a tree.*   Galatians 3:13

AMALEK AND ANCESTRAL STRUGGLES

Some families not only fight ancestral sins; they also fight the same circumstances, the same battles and the same struggles. Some families fight poverty from generation to generation, and no one in the family ever rises above the poverty line. There are those who fight and lose, and there are those who fight and win. The cursed will fight against their predicaments and lose, but the blessed will fight against their predicaments and win.

Abraham, Isaac, Jacob and Joseph all fought famine in their lifetime. Abraham escaped famine in Canaan by going to Egypt. He came back with plenty. Isaac stayed in the land during famine and sowed crops and reaped a hundred-fold harvest (see Genesis 26:12). Jacob and his children lived from the fat of Egypt during their seven years of famine. No doubt many perished in those days, but because God had promised to bless Abraham and his seed, famine could not prevail against them. May you, too, overcome ancestral battles in the name of Jesus!

For some, the struggle is against ancestral illnesses. Sarah, Abraham's wife was barren. Abraham battled with this until Sarah gave birth to Isaac, her only son. Then, Isaac's wife Rebecca also battled with barrenness. But Isaac prayed for her, and she was delivered. Jacob had this same struggle with his wife Rachel, but she also prevailed (although she died after giving birth to her second son, Benjamin).

Some families battle with cancer or other diseases. There are diseases that cannot be transferred physically through the bloodline, and yet somehow they are transferred to other generations. In other families, all the men go to jail or all the women remain single, even though they have a natural desire to marry. With other families, it does not matter how many opportunities are given to them, they never prosper. They just barely get along from day to day. With others, even though they exert much effort, the results are never anything worthwhile.

AMALEK AND RETALIATION

Amalek is a spirit of retaliation, and we have a mandate from God to war with it until it is totally removed from us. If Amalek is not warred against until it is completely destroyed, it will show up again somewhere in another generation, to fight against our descendants.

King Saul faced a King Amalek in his day too. God told Saul to totally destroy Amalek, but Saul spared him. Later, sometime during Israel's years of captivity, Amalek's descendant Haman rose up to retaliate against the people of Israel, to wipe them off the face of the earth (see 1 Samuel 15:2-20 and Esther 3:1-6). The enemies you refuse to destroy in your generation — the fight you refuse to fight and the battles you do not win — can rise up in another generation to fight against your descendants.

DEFEATING AMALEK

At the first encounter with Amalek, three elders of Israel (Moses, Aaron and Hur) went to the mountain to make intercession for Israel against Amalek. During the second encounter, King Saul and the prophet Samuel had to wage war against Amalek. In the third encounter, all Israel (including Queen Esther, her maids and her Uncle Mordecai) fasted and prayed to fight against Amalek. If you can get the elders of your family to fight against Amalek, that would be a good thing, and the entire family will benefit.

Ministering deliverance to an entire family is an awesome thing. It makes it easier for other family members to fight against Amalek and win. It is not easy to stand alone for your family, but Amalek can be defeated among your relations and in your own family line. You can cut your branch out of that family tree and attach or graft it into the True Vine, Jesus Christ. In this way, you can become a partaker of the seed of Jesse, and you can then claim your inheritance in Jesus Christ, the Son of God.

For if the firstfruit be holy, the lump is also holy: and if the root be holy, so are the branches. And if some of the branches be broken off, and thou, being a wild olive tree, wert grafted in among them, and with them partakest of the root and fatness of the olive tree ... . Romans 11:16-17

The lines are fallen unto me in pleasant places; yea, I have a goodly heritage. Psalm 16:6

You are an overcomer and a winner. You are greater than the weapons formed against you, so win every ancestral battle — in Jesus' name. Amen!

DESTROYING EVIL FOUNDATIONS PRAYER POINTS

◊ Repent and renounce every ancestral sin in your family (see Psalm 106:6).

◊ Ask the Lord for the blood of Jesus to cleanse your family from all ancestral sins (see 1 John 1:8-10).

◊ Break every ancestral curse in your family through the cross of Jesus (see Galatians 3:13-14).

◊ Bind and cast out every demonic spirit sent to enforce ancestral sins, illnesses and other calamities and mishaps in your family line (see Colossians 2:14-15).

◊ Graft your family branch to the Abrahamic Covenant blessings (see Romans 11:17).

◊ Receive the redemption and the inheritance that is in the blood of Jesus (see Ephesians 1:7-8).

◊ Thank the Lord and continue to fight the fight of faith, to lay hold of your promise in Christ Jesus (see 1 Timothy 6:12).

◊ Claim your heritage in the Root of David (see Psalm 16:6 and Revelation 22:16).

Chapter 2

APPROPRIATING BIBLICAL COVENANTS

For I say unto you, That except your righteousness shall exceed the righteousness of the scribes and Pharisees, ye shall in no case enter into the kingdom of heaven.
                                                    Matthew 5:20

WHAT IS APPROPRIATION?

One of the definitions of appropriation from *Dictionary.com* is: "the act of setting apart or taking for one's own use." The definition of appropriate is: "to take to or for oneself; take possession of" (late Latin 'appropriate': made one's own)." Jesus promised a lot of things in the New Testament to *"whosoever will,"* meaning whoever is willing to accept it as their own. If you don't believe in it and accept it as your own (even though God is still faithful to His Word and cannot deny Himself), it will have no effect on you. Those who decide to make it their own (in other words, appropriate them), possesses them:

He that believeth and is baptized shall be saved; but he that believeth not shall be damned. And these signs shall follow them that believe; In my name shall they cast out devils; they shall speak with new tongues; they shall take up serpents; and if they drink any deadly thing, it shall not hurt them; they shall lay hands on the sick, and they shall recover. Mark 16:16-18

You need to understand that the Word of God must be appropriated on the basis of faith. That is how God has ordained it. Believe and be saved; believe not and be damned (even though the provision has been made). God has ordained that those who want to come to Him to receive from Him on the bases of legal rights must come to Him on the basis of faith:

Behold, his soul which is lifted up is not upright in him: but the just shall live by his faith. Habakkuk 2:4

Now the just shall live by faith: but if any man draw back, my soul shall have no pleasure in him. Hebrews 10:38

But without faith it is impossible to please him: for he that cometh to God must believe that he is, and that he is a rewarder of them that diligently seek him.
Hebrews 11:6

You must appropriate the promises of God on the basis of faith.

We also escape the judgment of God by faith. If we do not believe in the salvation He has provided, we will be damned, condemned to be lost and in eternal punishment.

APPROPRIATING BIBLICAL COVENANTS

You cannot escape the judgment of God by simply not believing in it. He is the sovereign God, after all. If you do not believe (appropriating the salvation He has prepared for you), you will be condemned to eternal damnation, regardless of your religion or your denominational affiliation:

> *And he said unto them, Go ye into all the world, and preach the gospel to every creature. He that believeth and is baptized shall be saved; but he that believeth not shall be damned.* Mark 16:15-16

The Good News is that you can be saved from your sin, from eternal damnation, and from sickness, diseases, demonic dominion and bondages. The Good News is that you can partake of God's divine nature, ability and gifts. You can make it all yours on the basis of faith.

In this world of sin, wickedness, and demonic infestation, partaking of God's power, nature and ability is salvation. Not being a partaker of God's salvation means damnation in this life and the life to come. Hell can be experienced, both in this life and in the life to come. Heaven can be enjoyed, both in this life and in the life to come. For my part, I have eternal life, and I am living in Heaven right here on earth. It is the best life any man could ever dream of or imagine.

You do have a choice, and faith is that choice. If you do not believe, you will be damned. So, you have only one logical choice — FAITH. That is your only victory, and it is the victory for the whole world. Appropriate the Word of

God on the basis of faith, for there is no other way:

> *For whatsoever is born of God overcometh the world: and this is the victory that overcometh the world, even our faith. Who is he that overcometh the world, but he that believeth that Jesus is the Son of God?*   1 John 5:4-5

THE PRINCIPLE OF APPROPRIATION BY FAITH

The principle of appropriation by faith is express well in Romans Chapter 10:

> *But what does it say? The Word (God's message in Christ) is near you, on your lips and in your heart; that is, the Word (the message, the basis and object) of faith which we preach, because if you acknowledge and confess with your lips that Jesus is Lord and in your heart believe (adhere to, trust in, and rely on the truth) that God raised Him from the dead, you will be saved. For with the heart a person believes (adheres to, trusts in, and relies on Christ) and so is justified (declared righteous, acceptable to God), and with the mouth he confesses (declares openly and speaks out freely his faith) and confirms his salvation. The Scripture says, No man who believes in Him [who adheres to, relies on, and trusts in Him] will [ever] be put to shame or be disappointed.*   Romans 10:8-11, AMP

AN ACKNOWLEDGMENT OF THE LORDSHIP OF JESUS

This requires an acknowledgment on our part. According to the *Oxford Dictionary*, to *acknowledge* means "acceptance of the truth or existence of something." You need to acknowledge that Jesus Christ is Lord. He is the Lord of your life. You, as a person, belong to Him — in life and in death. His words, principles and prescribed ways for your life are the end of all argument and the basis for living, correction and instruction in righteousness.

Acknowledge that everything in Heaven, on earth and in the underworld must be subject to Him — whether they like it or not, for He is Lord of all. This is my knowledge in our Lord Jesus Christ and my confession of faith in Him. This is the WORD OF FAITH, which we preach in Christ Jesus.

ACKNOWLEDGEMENT THROUGH CONFESSION

What we believe we must then speak. Faith comes by HEARING, hearing the Word of God, and faith continues to grow by HEARING (present continuous tense) the Word of God (both the written Word, the Bible, and the spoken Word). Confess that Jesus Christ is Lord, repent of your sins and believe in Jesus' death, burial and resurrection for the remission of your sins, and you will be saved.

ACKNOWLEDGMENT THROUGH HEART BELIEVING

And shall not doubt in his heart, but shall believe that those things which he saith shall come to pass ...
Mark 11:23

The Scriptures say that we must believe with our heart. We cannot overemphasize BELIEF. Our acknowledging may begin from the head, but our believing must come from the heart. Head knowledge must become heart faith. Don't confess what you do not believe, for it will not work. You must believe that those things which you say will come to pass.

ACKNOWLEDGMENT THROUGH CORRESPONDING ACTION

Faith must be in the Word of God, faith must be in your heart and mouth, and faith must be in your actions:

> *Then Peter said, Silver and gold have I none; but such as I have give I thee: In the name of Jesus Christ of Nazareth rise up and walk. And he took him by the right hand, and lifted him up: and immediately his feet and ankle bones received strength. And he leaping up stood, and walked, and entered with them into the temple, walking, and leaping, and praising God.* Acts 3:6-8

YOU WILL NOT BE DISAPPOINTED

> *The Scripture says, No man who believes in Him [who adheres to, relies on, and trusts in Him] will [ever] be put to shame or be disappointed.* Romans 10:11, AMP

You will not be disappointed, and you will not be ashamed if you believe. Those who put their trust in the Lord shall not suffer these things. Your faith pleases God, and He watches over His Word to perform it. He is walking with us to confirm His Word with signs and wonders. His Word will not pass away unfulfilled. The Word of God abides forever. He is God, and He is Lord.

APPROPRIATING BIBLICAL COVENANTS

His Word is pure, and His Word is true. He esteems His Word even above His name. His Word is Himself, and He cannot deny Himself, for He is the living Word of God.

> *Heaven and earth shall pass away, but my words shall not pass away.*   Matthew 24:35

APPROPRIATING HEALING

All the promises of God through our redemption in Christ Jesus are appropriated on the basis of faith. You got saved by repenting of your sins and believing in the death, burial and resurrection of Jesus Christ from the dead for your righteousness. But being saved does not make you automatically healed of any illness you might have. Was healing part of your redemption? Yes, but in order to be healed, you have to appropriate your healing. How can you do that?

> *Is any sick among you? let him call for the elders of the church; and let them pray over him, anointing him with oil in the name of the Lord: and the prayer of faith shall save the sick, and the Lord shall raise him up; and if he have committed sins, they shall be forgiven him. Confess your faults one to another, and pray one for another, that ye may be healed.*   James 5:14-16

> *They shall take up serpents; and if they drink any deadly thing, it shall not hurt them; they shall lay hands on the sick, and they shall recover.*   Mark 16:18

So to appropriate your healing, first you must believe that healing is a part of your redemption. If you don't believe in divine healing and divine health, even though the provision is already made for your healing, it will not be yours. It is available, but you have not appropriated it; YOU HAVE NOT MADE IT YOUR OWN.

To make healing your own, you have to call for the elders of the church and let them anoint you with oil in the name of the Lord Jesus and pray the prayer of faith over you. If there are sins to confess, you will confess them, and then you will be healed. Or, find someone anointed to lay hands on you, and when they do, you will recover.

Sickness does not just run away from you when you get saved. Healing doesn't just fall into your lap when you accept Jesus as your Lord and Savior.

APPROPRIATING DELIVERANCE

The most misunderstood thought in the minds of many believers today is that once I am saved, I don't have any need for deliverance. It is like saying, "Once I am saved, I am also healed, because the promise is *'by whose stripes ye were healed'* (1 Peter 2:24)." Well, the fact is that you are healed, but you must appropriate it and then stand your ground to keep it. If you get sick, you must appropriate your healing, and if you are healed, you must appropriate divine health in order to stay healed.

Here are two passages that those who deny the need for further deliverance after salvation often quote:

APPROPRIATING BIBLICAL COVENANTS

Who hath delivered us from the power of darkness, and hath translated us into the kingdom of his dear Son: in whom we have redemption through his blood, even the forgiveness of sins. Colossians 1:13-14

Therefore if any man be in Christ, he is a new creature: old things are passed away; behold, all things are become new. And all things are of God, who hath reconciled us to himself by Jesus Christ, and hath given to us the ministry of reconciliation; to wit, that God was in Christ, reconciling the world unto himself, not imputing their trespasses unto them; and hath committed unto us the word of reconciliation. 2 Corinthians 5:17-19

I want to be quick to point out that these scriptures are true, to the saving of your spirit. No Christian can have a demon in his spirit. No! Your human spirit is where Jesus dwells, for God has made His abode there. But the Christian needs to have his mind renewed and transformed to the mind of Christ, and his body needs to be presented to God as a living sacrifice.

Some believers struggle in the areas of the flesh and the mind. They also struggle in other areas of their Christian living. They find that living the Christian life it is not as easy for them as it seems to be for others. They love the Lord dearly, but they are coming against forces stronger than can be overcome just by praying and fasting. Some will testify that fasting even seems to make their situation worse because the fasting further exposes it.

They have tried, "name it and claim it." They have tried "speaking the word" to it, "crucifying the flesh," "reckoning themselves indeed dead to sin," and "mortifying the deeds of the flesh," but nothing seems to work. This doesn't mean that the Word of God is of none effect; it just means that they have not yet applied the right principle to their problem.

All of these things will work if demonic entities are not involved, if you are just fighting the carnal mind and the sinful flesh. But if you are fighting demons, you must cast them out:

> *And these signs shall follow them that believe; In my name shall they cast out devils; they shall speak with new tongues.*   Mark 16:17

The deliverance ministry is a part of the healing ministry, and if healing can be appropriated after salvation from sins, then deliverance can also be imparted after you are saved. If there is sickness in your body when you are saved, you are not healed the moment you are saved, and in the same way demons will not leave your body the moment you get saved. They have to be ministered directly to, and that ministry is the deliverance ministry.

Jesus performed this ministry:

> *And Jesus went about all Galilee, teaching in their synagogues, and preaching the gospel of the kingdom, and healing all manner of sickness and all manner of disease among the people. And his fame went throughout all*

APPROPRIATING BIBLICAL COVENANTS

Syria: and they brought unto him all sick people that were taken with divers diseases and torments, and those which were possessed with devils, and those which were lunatick, and those that had the palsy; and he healed them.

Matthew 4:23-24

Jesus healed those who were possessed (taken with) demons and those who were lunatics. A believer cannot be possessed with a demon, but he can have a demon. But, praise the Lord, provision has been made for that. And, praise the Lord, it is part of our redemption. Believers do have demons, and our Lord Jesus Christ said that we should cast them out. Those who believe, He said, will cast out demons and speak with new tongues.

Just to make sure, once you have been saved, go for deliverance. Let any demons present be cast out, and then submit to the baptism of the Holy Spirit. Jesus said that demons should be cast out before we speak with tongues.

THE NEED FOR REPENTANCE

You must appropriate your deliverance. And how do you do that? You repent of all the sins you and your father's house and other ancestors have done to break the hedge God placed around you, for that allowed the enemy into your life. Put them all under the redemptive blood of Jesus Christ. This does not save your ancestors (if they have died in their sins); it just does not give the devil any legal ground to your life to do anything to you.

THE NEED FOR RENUNCIATION

Next, you need to renounce the enemy, and every covenant you and your ancestors have made with him and dispose of anything in your possession or in the possession of your household that belongs to Satan or his servants:

> *And many that believed came, and confessed, and shewed their deeds. Many of them also which used curious arts brought their books together, and burned them before all men: and they counted the price of them, and found it fifty thousand pieces of silver. So mightily grew the word of God and prevailed.* Acts 19:18-20

The Word of God grew and prevailed when the people disposed of the devilish things they had in their possession.

You cannot serve God's altar well when you have an altar to Satan still standing:

> *And it came to pass the same night, that the LORD said unto him, Take thy father's young bullock, even the second bullock of seven years old, and throw down the altar of Baal that thy father hath, and cut down the grove that is by it: and build an altar unto the LORD thy God upon the top of this rock, in the ordered place, and take the second bullock, and offer a burnt sacrifice with the wood of the grove which thou shalt cut down.* Judges 6:25-26

God told Jeremiah that He had set him over the nations and over the kingdoms and that there were things he had to do over the nations. He must first root out, pull down, destroy and throw down before he could start building and planting:

> *See, I have this day set thee over the nations and over the kingdoms, to root out, and to pull down, and to destroy, and to throw down, to build, and to plant.*
>
> Jeremiah 1:10

Unfortunately some of you have not dealt with the demonic altars still hanging over your heads, and whenever you begin to build and to plant, the enemy comes to kill your planting and destroy your building:

> *Behold Israel after the flesh: are not they which eat of the sacrifices partakers of the altar? What say I then? that the idol is any thing, or that which is offered in sacrifice to idols is any thing? But I say, that the things which the Gentiles sacrifice, they sacrifice to devils, and not to God: and I would not that ye should have fellowship with devils. Ye cannot drink the cup of the Lord, and the cup of devils: ye cannot be partakers of the Lord's table, and of the table of devils. Do we provoke the Lord to jealousy? are we stronger than he.*
>
> 1 Corinthians 10:18-22

THE NEED TO CAST THEM OUT

> *And these signs shall follow them that believe; In my name shall they cast out devils.*   Mark 16:17

Wherever these demonic powers are that have troubled you, drive them out. Use the weapons of your warfare against them. In the name of Jesus, they must leave. By the precious blood of Jesus, overcome them and go into warfare against them with your shield of faith and the Sword of the Spirit that is the Word of God. Resist the devil, and he will flee from you.

FIGHT THE FIGHT OF FAITH

There are those who do not believe in spiritual warfare. They don't believe we are at war and that there is a wrestling match going on between the Kingdom of God and the kingdom of the devil. The Bible, however, has warned us:

> *For we wrestle not against flesh and blood, but against principalities, against powers, against the rulers of the darkness of this world, against spiritual wickedness in high places. Wherefore take unto you the whole armour of God, that ye may be able to withstand in the evil day, and having done all, to stand.* Ephesians 6:12-13

> *Behold, I give unto you power to tread on serpents and scorpions, and over all the power of the enemy: and nothing shall by any means hurt you. Notwithstanding in this rejoice not, that the spirits are subject unto you; but rather rejoice, because your names are written in heaven.*
> Luke 10:19-20

Besides doing an initial deliverance for yourself, you need to understand that we are constantly engaging in spiritual warfare with the devil and his cohorts. You cannot afford to stand there doing nothing and just saying, "I am delivered from the powers of darkness," when the enemy is throwing his missiles at you. If you do not engage your weapons of warfare against the forces of darkness, you might get hit. Then you will suddenly begin to experience difficulties in your spiritual life and not know where they are coming from.

A MISCONCEPTION

There is a serious misconception afoot today that you can be delivered and the powers of darkness can renew the covenant without your consent and entrap and bind you again. This is nonsense. If that were the case, none of us would be delivered from the powers of darkness because those powers of darkness would have all of us bound regardless of what we did, and the blood of Jesus would not be sufficient to deliver us. That is rubbish:

As the bird by wandering, as the swallow by flying, so the curse causeless shall not come.   Proverbs 26:2

If the cause of a problem has been genuinely repented of, the blood of Jesus automatically cleanses us from all sins, and the devil has no occasion for inflicting us again for something we have done in the past that we have already been delivered from:

If we confess our sins, he is faithful and just to forgive us our sins, and to cleanse us from all unrighteousness. 1 John 1:9

USING POINTS OF CONTACT FOR APPROPRIATION

The promises of God are appropriated by means of what I call points of contact. These are things in the divine plan and order of God that bear spiritual significance. God has ordered them, and so we use them in faith to lay hold of the promises of His word. A *point of contact* can be defined as "a token, a signal, a flag, beacon, monument, omen, evidence, mark, miracle or sign." These marks or tokens carry spiritual significance with them.

We also need to understand that the kingdom of darkness uses the same points of contact that we use. You cannot judge the places you go only on the basis of points of contact. The spirit of deception has always been present, from the days of Balaam to the magicians of Pharaoh's to court and Ahab's prophets. Don't think that we are the same as them just because of similar points of contact. Here are some important points of contacts to remember:

BLOOD

In olden times, the blood of bulls, goats and birds was used, but now we are told to make no other blood covenant than with the blood of Jesus Christ, the Son of the living God.

IT IS FOR SALVATION FROM SINS

> *For the life of the flesh is in the blood: and I have given it to you upon the altar to make an atonement for your souls: for it is the blood that maketh an atonement for the soul.*   Leviticus 17:11

By the which will we are sanctified through the offering of the body of Jesus Christ once for all.
Hebrews 10:10

IT IS FOR PROTECTION AND WARFARE

The blood of Jesus does cry for mercy for the sinner, but at the same time, it is a weapon against the enemy. It is what we need to overcome the devil's temptations and wickedness:

And he said, What hast thou done? the voice of thy brother's blood crieth unto me from the ground. And now art thou cursed from the earth, which hath opened her mouth to receive thy brother's blood from thy hand;
Genesis 4:10-11

And they overcame him by the blood of the Lamb, and by the word of their testimony; and they loved not their lives unto the death.
Revelation 12:11

IT IS FOR POSSESSION OF A PROMISE

And he said, LORD God, whereby shall I know that I shall inherit it?
And he said unto him, Take me an heifer of three years old, and a she goat of three years old, and a ram of three years old, and a turtledove, and a young pigeon.
And he took unto him all these, and divided them in the midst, and laid each piece one against another: but the birds divided he not.
Genesis 15:8-10

Christ hath redeemed us from the curse of the law, being made a curse for us: for it is written, Cursed is every one that hangeth on a tree: that the blessing of Abraham might come on the Gentiles through Jesus Christ; that we might receive the promise of the Spirit through faith.

Galatians 3:13-14

IT IS FOR OWNERSHIP OF THE COVENANT

We do not believe that the circumcision of the flesh is necessary for New Testament believers, but the circumcision of the heart, otherwise called "the new creation":

Forasmuch as we have heard, that certain which went out from us have troubled you with words, subverting your souls, saying, Ye must be circumcised, and keep the law: to whom we gave no such commandment.

Acts 15:24

And ye shall circumcise the flesh of your foreskin; and it shall be a token of the covenant betwixt me and you.

Genesis 17:11

Ye shall not make any cuttings in your flesh for the dead, nor print any marks upon you: I am the Lord.

Leviticus 19:28

But he is a Jew, which is one inwardly; and circumcision is that of the heart, in the spirit, and not in the letter; whose praise is not of men, but of God.   Romans 2:29

APPROPRIATING BIBLICAL COVENANTS
IT IS FOR ETERNAL REDEMPTION

Neither by the blood of goats and calves, but by his own blood he entered in once into the holy place, having obtained eternal redemption for us. For if the blood of bulls and of goats, and the ashes of an heifer sprinkling the unclean, sanctifieth to the purifying of the flesh: and for this cause he is the mediator of the new testament, that by means of death, for the redemption of the transgressions that were under the first testament, they which are called might receive the promise of eternal inheritance.
Hebrews 9:12-15

For I have received of the Lord that which also I delivered unto you, That the Lord Jesus the same night in which he was betrayed took bread: and when he had given thanks, he brake it, and said, Take, eat: this is my body, which is broken for you: this do in remembrance of me. After the same manner also he took the cup, when he had supped, saying, This cup is the new testament in my blood: this do ye, as oft as ye drink it, in remembrance of me. For as often as ye eat this bread, and drink this cup, ye do shew the Lord's death till he come. 1 Corinthians 11:23-26

Sorcerers and other demonic instruments do other forms of blood covenants — from the making of incisions in the body of their followers to get blood, to the offering of animals and birds. If you go somewhere, and you are asked to do something like this, you can know that you are in the wrong place, and you need to get out of there fast. God said:

Ye shall not eat any thing with the blood: neither shall ye use enchantment, nor observe times
Ye shall not make any cuttings in your flesh for the dead, nor print any marks upon you: I am the LORD.
Leviticus 19:26 and 28

THE EARTH AND THE ATMOSPHERIC HEAVENS

Moses used dust to bring plagues on Egypt, turned water into blood and brought forth frogs from the water to punish the Egyptians. We also know that when Moses dropped his rod and it became a serpent, the magicians of Pharaoh's court did the same thing. They even turned water into blood. Today we are seeing sorcerers using cloths (red, black and white), fire, candles, ash, stones, salt etc., as points of contact to harm people.

When God made the triangular powers (sun, moon and stars), He placed them in the heavens for signs, seasons, days, years and nights. He also made them to rule the night and the day:

> *And God said, Let there be lights in the firmament of the heaven to divide the day from the night; and let them be for signs, and for seasons, and for days, and years: and let them be for lights in the firmament of the heaven to give light upon the earth: and it was so. And God made two great lights; the greater light to rule the day, and the lesser light to rule the night: he made the stars also. And God set them in the firmament of the heaven to give light upon the earth, and*

to rule over the day and over the night, and to divide the light from the darkness: and God saw that it was good.   Genesis 1:14-18

The triangular powers (sun, moon and stars) are used as points of contact to control and to change the times and seasons of people through witchcraft, Satanism and the occult. Worshipping solar and lunar powers and being involved with astrology and horoscope readings also opens doors to these demonic powers in the heavenlies.

God gave the stars of the sky and the sands of the seashore to Abraham as a sign, to remind him of His promise that he would be the father of multitude:

And he brought him forth abroad, and said, Look now toward heaven, and tell the stars, if thou be able to number them: and he said unto him, So shall thy seed be. And he believed in the LORD; *and he counted it to him for righteousness.*   Genesis 15:5-6

By observing the heavens, we can know if it will rain, snow or storm:

He answered and said unto them, When it is evening, ye say, It will be fair weather: for the sky is red. And in the morning, It will be foul weather to day: for the sky is red and lowring. O ye hypocrites, ye can discern the face of the sky; but can ye not discern the signs of the times?   Matthew 16:2-3

ASHES

And the LORD said unto Moses and unto Aaron, Take to you handfuls of ashes of the furnace, and let Moses sprinkle it toward the heaven in the sight of Pharaoh. And it shall become small dust in all the land of Egypt, and shall be a boil breaking forth with blains upon man, and upon beast, throughout all the land of Egypt. And they took ashes of the furnace, and stood before Pharaoh; and Moses sprinkled it up toward heaven; and it became a boil breaking forth with blains upon man, and upon beast.

Exodus 9:8-10

I am not suggesting that we use ashes as Moses did. He did what he did under the direct supervision of God. What I want to draw your attention to is that what Moses did sometimes the magicians of Pharaoh did also. The kingdom of darkness is also using these things, so in your warfare against demonic powers, you need to understand that this can become a weapon of darkness against you, to bring to pass the evil planned against you. It is a common thing for people in certain occultic practices in Africa, to blow ashes, and these carry demonic infirmities to inflict upon their victims. If you experience this when you are delivering people, come against it in Jesus' name.

OIL

Is any sick among you? let him call for the elders of the church; and let them pray over him, anointing him with oil in the name of the Lord: and the prayer of faith shall save the sick, and the Lord shall raise him up; and if he have committed sins, they shall be forgiven him.

James 5:14-15

Oil is also used as a point of contact for healing and for the consecration of ministers and kings. The oil symbolizes the anointing of the Lord for that individual, so that they can function in the particular ministry they are being anointed to function in.

MONEY

A feast is made for laughter, and wine maketh merry: but money answereth all things. Ecclesiastes 10:19

Every one that passeth among them that are numbered, from twenty years old and above, shall give an offering unto the LORD. The rich shall not give more, and the poor shall not give less than half a shekel, when they give an offering unto the LORD, to make an atonement for your souls. And thou shalt take the atonement money of the children of Israel, and shalt appoint it for the service of the tabernacle of the congregation; that it may be a memorial unto the children of Israel before the LORD, to make an atonement for your souls.

Exodus 30:14-16

Give, and it shall be given unto you; good measure, pressed down, and shaken together, and running over, shall men give into your bosom. For with the same measure that ye mete withal it shall be measured to you again.

Luke 6:38

Money is a seed. Everything can be converted to money because money is a means of exchange. Money can contract goods and services. Money is your life. Your time of service is converted to money, which is given to you as a wage. Through your offerings and tithes you contract prosperity. To get, you need to give, and your giving then becomes a point of contact to receive.

Sorcerers and false prophets also ask for money. Money can be used in payment to prophesy against you or curse you, to use enchantments against you or even kill you. The betrayal of our Lord Jesus by Judas was done for money. The chief priests called it *"blood money"* (Matthew 27:6, NIV). So, money is also a point of contact in the realms of the negative supernatural.

CLOTH OR CLOTHES AND THE JEWISH TALLIT

What is a *tallit*? The *tallit* (also pronounced tallis) is a prayer shawl, the most authentic Jewish garment. It is a rectangular-shaped piece of linen, wool, or silk with special fringes called *tzitzit* on each of the four corners. It became a point of contact for Israel with God:

> *The LORD said to Moses: Speak to the Israelites and instruct them to make for themselves fringes on the corners of their garments throughout the ages; let them attach a cord of blue to the fringe at each corner. That shall be*

*your fringe; look at it and recall all the commandments of the L*ORD *and observe them, so that you do not follow your heart and eyes in your lustful urge. Thus you shall be reminded to observe all my commandments and to be holy to your God.* Numbers 15:37-40

But unto you that fear my name shall the Sun of righteousness arise with healing in his wings; and ye shall go forth, and grow up as calves of the stall. Malachi 4:2

And God wrought special miracles by the hands of Paul: so that from his body were brought unto the sick handkerchiefs or aprons, and the diseases departed from them, and the evil spirits went out of them. Acts 19:11-12

And when the men of that place had knowledge of him, they sent out into all that country round about, and brought unto him all that were diseased; and besought him that they might only touch the hem of his garment: and as many as touched were made perfectly whole.
Matthew 14:35-36

And a woman having an issue of blood twelve years, which had spent all her living upon physicians, neither could be healed of any, came behind him, and touched the border of his garment: and immediately her issue of blood stanched. And Jesus said, Who touched me?
When all denied, Peter and they that were with him said, Master, the multitude throng thee and press thee, and sayest thou, Who touched me? Luke 8:43-45

All these scriptures show how the *tallit* and other clothes or handkerchiefs can be used as a point of contact to receive healing or blessing. It is also a common thing for Obeah men, or medicine men, to ask for clothes as a point of contact. The purveyors of witchcraft also uses clothes as a point of contact, to find and attack their victims. When we are praying for people for deliverance, one of the things we ask is if they have lost their undergarments or any other items of clothing mysteriously.

A lady adopted a young girl and started to take care of her, not knowing that she was a witch. Then one day her panties that she had worn while going through her menstrual cycle mysteriously disappeared. It turned out that the young girl had taken them to her witchcraft coven, and they had been used to afflict the woman with an infirmity.

Some people suddenly miss, not only items of clothing, but also jewelry or pieces of their hair, fingernails or toenails, and these items are being used as a point of contact in the realms of the powers of darkness to attack and afflict them. An effigy, in the form of a doll, much like a voodoo doll, has something belonging to them planted onto or into it, in order to attack them.

HANDS
AS A POINT OF CONTACT TO RECEIVE THE HOLY SPIRIT

Hands are used as a point of contact for believers in Christ to receive the Holy Spirit:

Saying, Give me also this power, that on whomsoever I lay hands, he may receive the Holy Ghost.   Acts 8:19

APPROPRIATING BIBLICAL COVENANTS

AS A POINT OF CONTACT TO RECEIVE HEALING

And these signs shall follow them that believe; In my name shall they cast out devils; they shall speak with new tongues; they shall take up serpents; and if they drink any deadly thing, it shall not hurt them; they shall lay hands on the sick, and they shall recover. Mark 16:17-18

AS POINT OF CONTACT TO RECEIVE A BLESSING

And Israel stretched out his right hand, and laid it upon Ephraim's head, who was the younger, and his left hand upon Manasseh's head, guiding his hands wittingly; for Manasseh was the firstborn. And he blessed Joseph, and said, God, before whom my fathers Abraham and Isaac did walk, the God which fed me all my life long unto this day. Genesis 48:14-15

Cults and occultic groups also anoint their adherents with oil and lay hands on them, but it is to transfer evil spirits to them and dedicate them to their occultic practices.

A SHADOW

And believers were the more added to the Lord, multitudes both of men and women. Insomuch that they brought forth the sick into the streets, and laid them on beds and couches, that at the least the shadow of Peter passing by might overshadow some of them. Acts 5:14-15

It is important to understand that the account of Peter's shadow healing the sick was an isolated instance. It was special. God is not stereotypical. He can use anything He wants as a point of contact. But we also need to understand that people actually did this. By faith, they brought their sick for Peter's shadow to rest on them, and it worked. There is no limit to where faith can go:

Then touched he their eyes, saying, According to your faith be it unto you. Matthew 9:29

A positive point of contact does not serve its own purpose. It serves whatever purpose God has given it. It carries God's anointing to bring about His desired work. You cannot, therefore, use a point of contact to manipulate people for money, and you cannot use one for a false purpose.

The kingdom of darkness also uses points of contact. They sometimes tell those who serve them to come with a number of fruits, stones or other things of significance that can be used to bind victims to their covenant.

God can work without any point of contact, and the righteous shall live by faith, but when He requires one, obey Him.

The people of Israel applied the blood to their doors and windows and were saved from the angel of death. In New Testament times, people received anointed handkerchiefs from the apostles, and they or their family members were healed. The New Testament disciples received the gift of the Holy Spirit by the laying on of hands. So a positive point of contact definitely does work.

APPROPRIATING BIBLICAL COVENANTS PRAYER POINTS

◊ Repent for every worship or consultation of triangular powers and renounce them.

◊ Repent of every worship of earth substances, animistic worship and practices and renounce them.

◊ Repent and renounce every belief and practice of the horoscope.

◊ Take authority and dominion over the triangular powers and every manipulation of them to alter your times and seasons and take control over your life (see Genesis 1:28).

◊ Take authority against any earth substance that is in use against you by the forces of darkness (see Genesis 1:29-30).

◊ If you have made any blood covenant, repent of it and renounce it in the name of Jesus. Ask the Lord to cleanse your blood by the blood of Jesus.

◊ Take authority against any demonic altar and blood bank of the devil, where your blood is being held, and release your life from those blood banks in Jesus' name.

◊ If you have made any human, animal, bird or even vegetable sacrifice, renounce it and break it in Jesus' name. Amen!

Chapter 3

DESTROYING DEMONIC STRONGHOLDS

For though we walk in the flesh, we do not war after the flesh: (for the weapons of our warfare are not carnal, but mighty through God to the pulling down of strong holds;) casting down imaginations, and every high thing that exalteth itself against the knowledge of God, and bringing into captivity every thought to the obedience of Christ; and having in a readiness to revenge all disobedience, when your obedience is fulfilled.   2 Corinthians 10:3-6

There can be no doubt that we Christians are in a spiritual war, and so our weapons of warfare must be spiritual weapons. I don't want to talk about the weapons of our warfare at this point, but, rather, the aspect of strongholds.

This passage directs itself to strongholds in the mind — imaginations, thoughts and disobedience. Sometimes we are tempted to limit negative strongholds to a faulty thinking pattern, a deception as to who God is and/or a deception as to who we are. But disobedience is also a cause of strongholds. Whatever their cause, negative strongholds are demonic, and they can be religious, geographical, territorial, political, cultural, mental, emotional and physical. Just as good strongholds are positions heavily guarded by God and His heavenly hosts, demonic strongholds are positions heavily guarded by Satan and his cohorts.

In ancient times, castles were erected as strongholds. They were positioned in strategic places to fortify against attacks from surrounding enemies. Such edifices were also sometimes called fortresses, citadels or garrisons. They were built with strong walls, strong gates and strong towers. Jesus, in teaching about a strongman and strongholds, said this:

> *When a strong man armed keepeth his palace, his goods are in peace: but when a stronger than he shall come upon him, and overcome him, he taketh from him all his armour wherein he trusted, and divideth his spoils. He that is not with me is against me: and he that gathereth not with me scattereth. When the unclean spirit is gone out of a man, he walketh through dry places, seeking rest; and finding none, he saith, I will return unto my house whence I came out. And when he cometh, he findeth it swept and garnished. Then goeth he, and taketh to him seven other spirits more wicked than himself; and they enter in, and dwell there: and the last state of that man is worse than the first.*   Luke 11:21-26

Strong men guard strongholds. The strong man of whom Jesus spoke is a Satanic personality who is usually fully armored to enable him to keep his palace or fortress.

He usually has other demons with him, helping him guard his castle. There might be legions of demons in such an evil garrison, so that it becomes a stronghold. Satan is determined to keep his captives at all costs:

> *For he said unto him, Come out of the man, thou unclean spirit. And he asked him, what is thy name?*
> *And he answered, saying, My name is Legion: for we are many. And he besought him much that he would not send them away out of the country.* Mark 5:8-10

All demonic strongholds and strong men were defeated on the cross of Jesus Christ. He overcame them a long time ago and gave us authority over them. So, take them as your captives, in Jesus' name:

> *Wherefore he saith, When he ascended up on high, he led captivity captive, and gave gifts unto men. (Now that he ascended, what is it but that he also descended first into the lower parts of the earth? He that descended is the same also that ascended up far above all heavens, that he might fill all things.)* Ephesians 4:8-10

THE ANNOUNCEMENT OF THE KINGDOM OF GOD

Both Jesus and John came preaching the Kingdom of God:

> *In those days came John the Baptist, preaching in the wilderness of Judaea, and saying, Repent ye: for the kingdom of heaven is at hand.* Matthew 3:1-2

BREAKING DOWN STRONGHOLDS

From that time Jesus began to preach, and to say, Repent: for the kingdom of heaven is at hand.   Matthew 4:17

From the days of John, the Kingdom of God has suffered violence from the kingdom of darkness — the reaction of religious spirits, violence (the killing of John and the persecution of Jesus) and demons popping up here and there:

And from the days of John the Baptist until now the kingdom of heaven suffereth violence, and the violent take it by force.   Matthew 11:12

The announcement of the Kingdom of Heaven by John the Baptist and by our Lord Jesus Christ brought on a rage from the elements of the kingdom of darkness against us. Satan knows that the Kingdom of God will bring his kingdom down, so from that time, he has been raging violently against God's Kingdom. But the Kingdom of God is forcefully advancing, because violent men and women are taking the kingdom of darkness by force. Why not join in the fight against all the forces of darkness, just as Jesus did in His day.

It does not matter what country you are a citizen of; there are only two kingdoms on the earth. You are either a citizen of the Kingdom of God or a citizen of the kingdom of darkness. And these two kingdoms are at war with each other. You are either with Jesus or against Him. Not being *with* Jesus means that you have already made a decision for the other side:

> *He that is not with me is against me; and he that gathereth not with me scattereth abroad.*   Matthew 12:30

SIGNS OF THE KINGDOM

> *But if I with the finger of God cast out devils, no doubt the kingdom of God is come upon you.*   Luke 11:20

The act of Jesus driving out demons by the finger of God was proof that the Kingdom of Heaven was here. When the king of darkness and his kingdom were in power, everyone was subject to them, but when the Kingdom of Heaven came, all the authorities of the kingdom of darkness had to become subject to the Kingdom of God:

> *He that committeth sin is of the devil; for the devil sinneth from the beginning. For this purpose the Son of God was manifested, that he might destroy the works of the devil.*
>   1 John 3:8

The purpose of Jesus' coming down as a shinning light to this earth was to destroy Satan's kingdom, causing it to fall:

> *And he said unto them, I beheld Satan as lightning fall from heaven. Behold, I give unto you power to tread on serpents and scorpions, and over all the power of the enemy: and nothing shall by any means hurt you. Notwithstanding in this rejoice not, that the spirits are subject unto you; but rather rejoice, because your names are written in heaven.*   Luke 10:18-20

The Kingdom of God is itself a stronghold. Jesus said:

I will build my church and the gates of hell shall not prevail against it.   Matthew 16:18

We are stronger than the devil. The prophet Nahum declared:

The LORD is good, a strong hold in the day of trouble; and he knoweth them that trust in him.   Nahum 1:7

The Lord is our stronghold against the forces of darkness, and with Him are *"an innumerable company of angels"*:

But ye are come unto mount Sion, and unto the city of the living God, the heavenly Jerusalem, and to an innumerable company of angels.   Hebrews 12:22

As the apostolic leader of several ministries, my work has been to go and break up the ground for churches to be planted in new areas. In the course of this work, I have been to what I would call demonic towns and villages, places where no Bible-believing churches have ever been planted. These are places where sorcery and witchcraft are the principalities and powers and ruling spirits. So the warfare I have had to take on has been great. Demons have attacked us in our dreams, attacked our finances and equipment, and they have tried to attack us physically. For certain they have conspired against us, and, at times, we have had to spend all night praying to overcome them. Witches have come to our meetings, but God exposed them, and they were forced to confess their sins.

In one village, a python spirit was in charge. People reported seeing it at the entrance of the village. Immediately they told it to fall to the ground and die. Many of the young girls in that village were married to river spirits. Some of the members of the liberal churches there, before our coming, had been members of the occult and some were even witches. But, praise the Lord, we were able to pull down the demonic strongman and stronghold over that village through our intercessory and deliverance crusades, and today there are more than fifty Bible-practicing evangelical and Pentecostal churches there. There is even a Christian retreat center there. That place, that once was a stronghold for Satan, is now a stronghold for God.

I am aware that some readers in the West may find these examples to be farfetched, superstitious or medieval, but I can assure you that in much of Africa, Asia and South America, these occult experiences are part of the everyday reality.

There is a strongman over your city. He may even have his stronghold located on your street. Witches, wizards, violence, drugs, prostitution, immorality and drunkenness control many cities, and believers are trying to take those cities without first going into warfare against these forces. Many believers are too shy to mention demons of prostitution or demons of drug addiction. They pray other kinds of prayers, when they should be driving out those demons from the lives of the people.

If demons remain unchallenged and continue to have their way (because believers are afraid to mention demons), this fortifies their stronghold. In many of our churches today, if people come in who have demons and there is some small manifestation of these spirits, these people are quickly removed from the church sanctuary and taken to some back room. Why? Because most of the members of the churches there are ignorant concerning spiritual warfare. If pastors are guilty of not teaching these things, it may well be because they are also ignorant of them.

As a whole, the church is now much too modernized to drive out demons, so many demonic cases are now reclassified as "psychological problems." The result is that many are in jail or in mental hospitals when they could have been set free long ago — if a pastor or a believer had known how to drive out demons.

Many pastors consider it to be an embarrassment to them and to their people to mention demons, and, because they are afraid to lose people, they try never to mention evil spirits. The result is that they lose their people anyway, but they lose them to the demons. God said in His Word:

> *Lest Satan should get an advantage of us: for we are not ignorant of his devices.* 2 Corinthians 2:11

> *My people are destroyed for lack of knowledge: ... thou hast rejected knowledge ... .* Hosea 4:6

DESTROYING DEMONIC STRONGHOLDS PRAYER POINTS

- ◊ Bind the strongman in charge over the situation (see Mark 3:27).

- ◊ Pray for the spirit of might and boldness against the powers of darkness (see Acts 4:6 and Isaiah 11:2).

- ◊ Pray for the signs of the Kingdom to follow you and your ministry, in Jesus' name (see Mark 16:17).

- ◊ Pray for the gifts of the Spirit to be operational in your life, especially the gift of discerning of spirits and the gift of healing (see 1 Corinthians 12:9).

- ◊ Use your spiritual authority against the powers of the enemy (see Luke 10:19).

- ◊ Use the weapons of your warfare (see 2 Corinthians 10:4-6 and Ephesians 6:15-18).

CHAPTER 4

YOU CANNOT SERVE TWO MASTERS

Be ye not unequally yoked together with unbelievers: for what fellowship hath righteousness with unrighteousness? and what communion hath light with darkness? And what concord hath Christ with Belial? or what part hath he that believeth with an infidel? And what agreement hath the temple of God with idols? for ye are the temple of the living God; as God hath said, I will dwell in them, and walk in them; and I will be their God, and they shall be my people. Wherefore come out from among them, and be ye separate, saith the Lord, and touch not the unclean thing; and I will receive you, And will be a Father unto you, and ye shall be my sons and daughters, saith the Lord Almighty. 2 Corinthians 6:14-18

Here we find two very important questions: "*What concord hath Christ with Belial?*" and "*What agreement hath the temple of God with idols?*" Christ has no harmony or agreement with the devil. They do not dance to the same music, nor do they join themselves in the any endeavor. They do not dance to the same beat. Christ and Satan don't mix. The word *belial*, as used here, is a term used for a worthless person. Christ has no dealing with worthlessness.

There is a widely-circulated argument that "all roads lead to God." No, that's not true! Not all roads lead to God. Not all religions lead to God, and certainly not all that is worshipped is God. People may think they are worshipping God, but behind their worship is a devil:

> *But I say, that the things which the Gentiles sacrifice, they sacrifice to devils, and not to God: and I would not that ye should have fellowship with devils. Ye cannot drink the cup of the Lord, and the cup of devils: ye cannot be partakers of the Lord's table, and of the table of devils. Do we provoke the Lord to jealousy? are we stronger than he.*   1 Corinthians 10:20-22

You cannot profess Christianity and, at the same time, be a member of Free Masonry or other fraternities, or Palo Mayombe, [1] Santería [2] or Macumba. [3] You cannot

---
1. A group of closely related religions which developed in the Spanish Empire among Central African slaves who originated in the Congo region. The branches of Palo include Mayombe (or Mallombe), Monte, Briyumba (or Brillumba), and Kimbisa (https://en.wikipedia.org/wiki/Palo_(religion)).
2. A syncretic religion of Caribbean origin which developed in the Spanish Empire among West African slaves. Influenced by and syncretized with Roman Catholicism, it is a system of beliefs that merges aspects of Yoruba mythology, which were brought to the New World by Yoruba slaves, with Christianity and Indigenous American traditions. The slaves carried with them various religious customs, including a trance and divination system for communicating with their ancestors and deities, animal sacrifice, and sacred drumming and dance (https://en.wikipedia.org/wiki/Santería).
3. A Brazilian cult incorporating the use of fetishes and sorcery and deriving largely from African practices (http://dictionary.com).

profess Christianity and, at the same time, belong to the Occult or visit an Obeah Man [4] or visit a Medicine Man, or practice Voodoo or be a witch or wizard. You cannot profess Christianity and read tarot cards or visit or practice Necromancy, or believe in Astrology or the Horoscope or practice ancestral worship and the worship of idols.

The Scriptures say that you should come out from among them and not touch these unclean things if the Lord is to receive you and be a Father to you and for you to become His sons and daughters:

Wherefore come out from among them, and be ye separate, saith the Lord, and touch not the unclean thing; and I will receive you. And will be a Father unto you, and ye shall be my sons and daughters, saith the Lord Almighty.

2 Corinthians 6:17-18

THE TEMPLE OF GOD VS IDOLS

What agreement hath the temple of God with idols?"

I want to look at certain fundamental aspects of these religious and occult practices that make them

---

[4]. Sometimes spelled Obi, Obea or Obia, it is a term used in the West Indies to refer to folk magic, sorcery and religious practices developed among West African slaves, specifically of Igbo origin. Obeah is similar to other Afro-American religions including Palo, Vodou, Santería, and Hoodoo. Obeah is practiced in Suriname, Cuba, Jamaica, Trinidad and Tobago, Dominica, Guyana, Barbados, Grenada, Belize, the Bahamas and other Caribbean nations (https://en.wikipedia.org/wiki/Obeah). In some cultures, the Obeah Man is known as the Medicine Man.

incompatible with Christ. Attempting to live the Christian life and continue to practice these things is a contradiction. Why did God say that we must be separated from them and touch nothing that has to deal with them?

With many of these kinds of practices comes an initiation ceremony which is a sort of "new birth" or "a spiritual marriage" and they require swearing an oath. Some of them have spiritual bathing, a blood covenant and/or a covenant meal to be shared. Concerning this, God said:

> *But I say, that the things which the Gentiles sacrifice, they sacrifice to devils, and not to God: and I would not that ye should have fellowship with devils. Ye cannot drink the cup of the Lord, and the cup of devils: ye cannot be partakers of the Lord's table, and of the table of devils. Do we provoke the Lord to jealousy? are we stronger than he.*
>
> 1 Corinthians 10:20-22

There are many good reasons that God has warned us not to become part of these practices:

SECRECY

> *Jesus answered him, I spake openly to the world; I ever taught in the synagogue, and in the temple, whither the Jews always resort; and in secret have I said nothing. Why askest thou me? ask them which heard me, what I have said unto them: behold, they know what I said.*
>
> John 18:20-21

YOU CANNOT SERVE TWO MASTERS

Any group that has secret practices, something hidden from the public view, is not of God. And any time you are required to put yourself under an oath to never reveal such hidden aspects (sometimes to the point of pronouncing a curse on yourself if you do), this is a cult or an occult practice and you should have nothing to do with it — even if the practitioners sometimes call on the name of Jesus:

> *Not every one that saith unto me, Lord, Lord, shall enter into the kingdom of heaven; but he that doeth the will of my Father which is in heaven.*   Matthew 7:21

Freemasonry is one of the groups that has a secret initiation. All that we need for life and godliness is revealed to us in the Bible, which is made available to all. You need no secret book and no other form of enlightenment. Believe me, if you accept secret practices, you are dabbling with darkness. You are no poor blind beggar looking from darkness into the light of Freemasonry. The very fact that you must be blindfolded to join such an order and that a dagger is placed on your chest as you pronounce death on yourself for ever revealing their secrets is all an indication that this is not a group you should want to belong to as a Christian. But taking such an oath, you may well be pronouncing a curse of death upon yourself.

SPIRITUAL MARRIAGE

> *For the woman which hath a husband is bound by the law to her husband so long as he liveth; but if the husband be*

dead, she is loosed from the law of her husband. So then if, while her husband liveth, she be married to another man, she shall be called an adulteress: but if her husband be dead, she is free from that law; so that she is no adulteress, though she be married to another man. Romans 7:2-3

Most of these false religions or practices have some sort of spiritual marriage attached to them. As Christians, we are called the Bride of Christ. If you are married to Christ and have not divorced Him, then why are you marrying someone else? In God's eyes, you are now an adulterer.

In Freemasonry, a ring is placed on your fourth finger, which is a symbol of marriage. The collars, the gauntlets, and the apron, with its snake clasp, balls and chains, are all elements to hold you to that marriage.

In Santería, you enter a spiritual marriage and become the iyawó or "bride" of Orisha, and this is the case with many other religions in the world today. In some cults, you are initiated into them through sexual union or by being given a ring or being married to a demon.

A YOUNG GIRL'S STORY

A mother took her young primary school girl to an occultist priest for protection from pregnancy. The place they lived in was ruled by a strong spirit of immorality, and most of the young girls ended up pregnant and had to drop out of school. This mother wanted her child to learn and to go on to university, so she did what she knew to do to help her.

YOU CANNOT SERVE TWO MASTERS

The Medicine Man or Obeah Man gave her a chain he had made out of beads to wear around her waist, and it seemed to help. Back home, the girl now seemed to have lost all interest in boys. She had no time for them. All she had time for was her school work. But, from the time she began to wear the beads, she began to dream each night that a man would come and have sex with her.

She went on to the university and, in many ways, seemed to be proceeding as normal. Like most girls her age, she had boyfriends, but any time the relationship began to get too intimate, she would break it off.

After she had finished her university studies, her problems began. As was the custom, a marriage was arranged for her, and since she had no choice in the matter, she married and submitted to sex with her husband. But, she later confessed, it was the most painful thing she had ever experienced. It was not that the man was being rough with her; it was that she had been spoiled with her relationship with the man of her dreams. He continued to come to her each night and their union was the most pleasurable thing she could ever imagine.

No one else knew, but as the child got older and began to outgrow the beaded waist band, from time to time the mother would take it back to the Medicine Man, and he would lengthen it and renew the covenant marriage with the girl. After years of this terrible experience, the girl, now a lady, came to us for deliverance. She knew that she needed help.

As we started to pray for her, her whole countenance began to change. Her pupils began to dilate, and her eyes became fixed. There was no blink of her eyelid, even it you pretended to poke her in the eye. Her voice also changed, and she began to speak with a male voice. The demon n her then told the story of how he had married her as a child and how he was the legal husband. We then commanded the demon to leave her, as all legal rights were now broken.

Did I say "all"? No! There was still one element left. We had no way of knowing that the lady was still wearing the beaded waist cord that had started it all. The power of God now ran through her body, and His fire began to burn that chain around her waist. She screamed, "Fire!" Then she reached into her skirt and pulled out the offending beaded chain, and she was delivered. She had been having difficulty having children, but after the deliverance she gave birth. Praise the Lord! Another soul delivered.

BLOOD COVENANTS

Many of these religions and occultic practices involve blood covenants. Just as in Christianity, where the blood of Jesus Christ saves us, heals us, delivers and protects us, many false religions practice other types of blood covenants. These include Palo and Santería.

Incisions are made somewhere in the body or some Medicine Man will tell you to offer the sacrifice of a chicken, a cow, a goat or a sheep. This is true of Voodoo. With Palo, you are given a pot with demons in it, and you must offer a chicken as a sacrifice. The Scriptures warn us to abstain from all such practices:

YOU CANNOT SERVE TWO MASTERS

As touching the Gentiles which believe, we have written and concluded that they observe no such thing, save only that they keep themselves from things offered to idols, and from blood, and from strangled, and from fornication.
Acts 21:25

COME OUT FROM AMONG THEM

We are to *"come out from among them"*:

Wherefore come out from among them, and be ye separate, saith the Lord, and touch not the unclean thing; and I will receive you, and will be a Father unto you, and ye shall be my sons and daughters, saith the Lord Almighty.
2 Corinthians 6:17-19

This is not a new thing that God is calling His Church out of. When He called Israel, He had to tell them not to practice such things.

The practitioners of Freemasonry, for example, pledge oaths to witchcraft, Baalim and ancient Egyptian, Babylonian, Chaldean and Chinese gods. They worship a multitude of gods, so Freemasonry is clearly idolatry. You need to come out from among them and have nothing to do with them. If you have anything to do with them, God has rejected you, and you are no longer His child. These are all false religions in disguise. If you are wise, you will run from them.

The practice of transcendental meditation and yoga is not just an art to relax your brain and muscles, as many now claim. These are all a part of the practices of Eastern-based religions. Don't have anything to do with them. Don't chant their mantras. Whatever anyone tells you, you are not just making sounds. Every sound has an interpretation. If you don't know the meaning of a word or sound, don't say it. There is too much at risk:

> *And even things without life giving sound, whether pipe or harp, except they give a distinction in the sounds, how shall it be known what is piped or harped? For if the trumpet give an uncertain sound, who shall prepare himself to the battle? So likewise ye, except ye utter by the tongue words easy to be understood, how shall it be known what is spoken? for ye shall speak into the air. There are, it may be, so many kinds of voices in the world, and none of them is without signification. Therefore if I know not the meaning of the voice, I shall be unto him that speaketh a barbarian, and he that speaketh shall be a barbarian unto me.* 1 Corinthians 14:7-11

RENOUNCING NEGATIVE MASTERS PRAYER POINTS

Here are some steps toward deliverance from the occult and false religions. Take them one-by-one in faith and receive a complete breakthrough in Jesus' name. Amen!

- ◊ Repent.
- ◊ Renounce their gods.
- ◊ Renounce their oaths.
- ◊ Revoke all blood covenants.
- ◊ Break the marriage.
- ◊ Put off their armor.
- ◊ Denounce their new birth.
- ◊ Cleanse yourself by the blood of Jesus from all ceremonial baths.
- ◊ Break their curses.
- ◊ Burn all their belongings with fire.
- ◊ Stop paying all pledges and allegiances to them.
- ◊ Constantly engage in spiritual warfare against them.

CHAPTER 5

DESTROYING RELIGIOUS STRONGHOLDS

But there were false prophets also among the people, even as there shall be false teachers among you, who privily shall bring in damnable heresies, even denying the Lord that bought them, and bring upon themselves swift destruction. And many shall follow their pernicious ways; by reason of whom the way of truth shall be evil spoken of. And through covetousness shall they with feigned words make merchandise of you: whose judgment now of a long time lingereth not, and their damnation slumbereth not.
2 Peter 2:1-3

There are different categories of demonic strongholds, from the strongholds in an individual's life, leading to family strongholds which end up as generational strongholds, to strongholds over geographical, territorial, religious and political sectors. Let us now look at these kinds of strongholds and see how demonic strongmen guard those who are under their control and how their victims can be freed. These strongholds include the following:

RELIGIOUS STRONGHOLDS

I would define religion as "a faith, a belief system, and a kind of worship and confession of creed in honor to and in respect of a god." Lucifer was once called *"the anointed cherub that covereth"* (Ezekiel 28:14). He was a cherub (angelic being) who was in charge of worship in Heaven (see verses 13-15). However, it became his quest to receive worship instead of God and his pride and covetousness of God's throne led to his downfall. Now, he is the author of all false religions, cults and occultic practices that give him the worship he requires:

And no marvel; for Satan himself is transformed into an angel of light.   2 Corinthians 11:14

There are so many erroneous teachings about God in the world today. False religions around the world include Islam, Hinduism, Shintoism, Confucianism, Taoism, Baha'i, Sikhism, Ancestral Worship, Santería, Palo Mayombe, Voodoo, Macumba, Umbanda, [5] Candomblé, [6] just to name a few. Some of these religions originated with a visitation from a personage (a religious spirit) to their prophets. Other religions came out of another religion, and others still have been syncretized with Catholicism, Protestantism, Islam or some other major religion. All of

---

5. A syncretic Brazilian religion that blends African traditions with Roman Catholicism, Spiritism, and Indigenous American beliefs (https://en.wikipedia.org/wiki/Umbanda).
6. A religion based on African beliefs which is particularly popular in Brazil. It is also practiced in other countries and has as many as two million followers (https://en.wikipedia.org/wiki/Candomblé)..

these religions have demonic origins, and they all propagate a salvation from a means other than salvation by grace through faith in Jesus Christ. They all go about finding their own righteousness, other than the righteousness that Christ gives:

> *For they being ignorant of God's righteousness, and going about to establish their own righteousness, have not submitted themselves unto the righteousness of God. For Christ is the end of the law for righteousness to every one that believeth.* Romans 10:3-4

Teachings like pantheism, reincarnation, humanism, syncretism, paganism, Satanism, yoga and all their practices are all deception and represent worship given to Satan and not to God. Even much of the belief systems and practices of churches like the Unification Church, the Mormons and the Catholic Church can be traced to deceptive religious spirits.

There are also religious spirits within conservative Christianity itself, and these religious spirits have built strongholds in every denomination from Protestantism to Evangelical Christianity, Pentecostalism and the Charismatic renewal. All have religious spirits with strongholds of belief systems and practices that are out of order. There are groups within all of these sets of Christianity that have opened themselves to these seducing spirits:

> *Now the Spirit speaketh expressly, that in the latter times some shall depart from the faith, giving heed to seducing*

spirits, and doctrines of devils; speaking lies in hypocrisy; having their conscience seared with a hot iron; forbidding to marry, and commanding to abstain from meats, which God hath created to be received with thanksgiving of them which believe and know the truth. 1 Timothy 4:1-3

Seducing spirits are responsible for religious strongholds. They propagate demonic doctrines. Some teachings, though erroneous, do not cause us to lose eternity, but others are more serious, causing many to depart from the faith and to lose their eternal life.

Some teachings have no scriptural backing at all, while others are based on a misinterpretation of the Scriptures. Whether the erroneous teaching is a result of a seducing spirit or a mere misunderstanding of scripture, those religious strongholds must be pulled down from the minds and spirits of those who are held by them.

The deceptions common in the church vary a lot, from laws concerning apparel, to foods not to eat or the observance of certain days and feasts. Some churches have cut themselves off from other believers under the deception that they alone are right, and all others are wrong. Some believe that their prophet is right and all others are false. These teachings build strongholds in the minds of the people, to hook and then hold them bound in their churches.

SIGNS OF RELIGIOUS SPIRITS

Any professed faith that uses other books than the Bible or that depend solely on other book to interpret the Holy Scriptures is inspired and guided by religious spirits.

DESTROYING RELIGIOUS STRONGHOLDS

Any Christian groups that believe that their church alone saves and gives absolution and all others are in error is dominated by religious spirits. Any church that carries the belief system that only their spiritual leader has the whole truth and are forbidden to listen to other preachers or visit other churches is controlled by religious spirits. Any church that threatens you with a curse if you leave them is dominated by religious spirits, and such beliefs have built strongholds in the minds of their people, and they need to be delivered from them. Heresy, according to Paul in the book of Galatians, is a work of the flesh, and it can prevent entrance into the Kingdom of God (see Galatians 5:19-21).

Some fight more for their distinctive practices than they do for the Lord Jesus Himself. They are willing to fight for their baptismal formula, even if it means losing a brother. Others fight for the observance of days and years and feasts or for clean and unclean meats or dress codes, making them a means for salvation alongside of the atoning death, burial and resurrection of Jesus. Whenever we see this, we can know that there are very strong religious spirits at work. We are saved by grace through faith alone:

For by grace are ye saved through faith; and that not of yourselves: it is the gift of God. Ephesians 2:8

Other groups are under strong legalistic and mystical practices, which hold them in bondage. They are governed by a host of rules and regulations. As a result, many have lost the love of God and the liberty that Christ gives. Their worship is no longer governed by a love for Christ.

It is now fear that holds them in bondage. Paul wrote to the Galatian believers:

> *Stand fast therefore in the liberty wherewith Christ hath made us free, and be not entangled again with the yoke of bondage.*   Galatians 5:1

Amen!

DESTROYING RELIGIOUS STRONGHOLDS PRAYER POINTS

- ◊ Repent for holding such erroneous teachings and imposing them on others (see Mark 1:15).

- ◊ Renounce and bind the seducing spirits that have lured you into such a belief system, in Jesus' name (see 1 Timothy 4:1).

- ◊ Bind witchcraft spirits of control over such a belief system, in Jesus' name (see Galatians 3:1).

- ◊ Bind every lying spirit and release yourself from the spirit of delusion, in Jesus' name (see 2 Thessalonians 2:11).

- ◊ Cast down those belief systems and all their imaginations and thoughts and bring them into captivity to the obedience of Christ (see 2 Corinthians 10:5).

- ◊ Pray for transformation through the renewing of your mind (see Romans 12:2).

- ◊ Meditate on the Word of God (see Joshua 1:8).

Chapter 6

DESTROYING SPIRITUAL PROSTITUTION

And if the people of the land do any ways hide their eyes from the man, when he giveth of his seed unto Molech, and kill him not: then I will set my face against that man, and against his family, and will cut him off, and all that go a whoring after him, to commit whoredom with Molech, from among their people. And the soul that turneth after such as have familiar spirits, and after wizards, to go a whoring after them, I will even set my face against that soul, and will cut him off from among his people.

Leviticus 20:4-6

There are people who seem to be programed in the negative supernatural to prostitute from one demonic group to another. For some, the same pattern occurs even once they are saved. They move from church to church and never settle down anywhere. Some end up in a cult. Others still are prone to move from one cult to another. They never find what they are looking for.

Some people, even though they have become Christians, are still prone to go to fortune-tellers and tarot card readers. Some might not go to those who are outside the faith, but they will prostitute themselves from one prophet to another prophet. It is sad to say that some of the so-called prophets at work today are themselves users of divination and fortune telling. They have the spirit of Balaam.

THE SPIRIT OF BALAAM

> *And Israel abode in Shittim, and the people began to commit whoredom with the daughters of Moab. And they called the people unto the sacrifices of their gods: and the people did eat, and bowed down to their gods. And Israel joined himself unto Baalpeor: and the anger of the LORD was kindled against Israel. And the LORD said unto Moses, Take all the heads of the people, and hang them up before the LORD against the sun, that the fierce anger of the LORD may be turned away from Israel. And Moses said unto the judges of Israel, Slay ye every one his men that were joined unto Baalpeor.*   Numbers 25:1-5

Balaam used every kind of divination to curse Israel, but he could not. The only way he could get to the people of Israel was to get them to start sinning against God. He got them to be unequally yoked with the daughters of Moab, and in that process, they were invited to the local feasts and the sacrifice to the local gods. In this way, the men of Israel eventually prostituted themselves before the Moabite gods.

This has been a powerful weapon in the hands of the devil for many ages. We see that the same happened with the mighty Samson (mighty until Delilah), and with the otherwise wise Solomon (and his many strange wives). With Ahab, it was Jezebel. Some people are programed in the demonic realms to always meet partners who dabble in the negative supernatural. Somehow it does not matter where they go, they always end up in a relationship with the wrong kind of people. It is my observation that although these people appear outwardly spiritual, they live carnally. Still, they either claim to hear God's word, prophesy, or see a vision for you to follow. The word these people receive never exposes the people's sins, but tells them how prosperous they will become.

These days it is common for the spirit of spiritual prostitution to tell you that the church you are in is not your church, and your pastor is not your "spiritual covering." Some today have moved from church to church in search of their so-called spiritual covering. This has caused a lot of church splits and rivalry and bitterness between pastors. Some of these people even come to your church and prophesy to your members. Church members who cannot commit to one church can either be a carrier of that spirit or are prone to catch that spirit:

> *They sacrifice upon the tops of the mountains, and burn incense upon the hills, under oaks and poplars and elms, because the shadow thereof is good: therefore your daughters shall commit whoredom, and your spouses shall commit adultery. I will not punish your daughters when they commit whoredom, nor your spouses when they commit adultery: for themselves are separated with whores, and*

they sacrifice with harlots: therefore the people that doth not understand shall fall.   Hosea 4:13-14

RUNAWAYS

There are people the devil has programed for spiritual prostitution through their parents or even grandparents who were involved with the occult. This spirit takes its toll on their marital and spiritual life. Often it merges with their marriage and spiritual and political lives. Some people are in their second or third marriage and already want out.

Some Christians are in and out of Christianity and back and forth from one religion to another. Others move from church to church and are prone to move on quickly. They never find their so-called spiritual covering. They are always quick to listen to prophets who tell them they have not found their true spiritual covering. They receive some prophecies that agree and others that disagree with their feelings. Therefore they are always left confused, sometimes on a spiritual high and, at other times, on a spiritual low.

Many times they feel threatened by others in the church, always feeling that someone in the church is dabbling with the powers of darkness to hurt them. They always have some kind of reason for leaving one church for another, only to find things repeating themselves in the next church they enter. It's called spiritual prostitution.

There is no security in a marriage with such people. If they tell you about their past, you will feel sympathy for them, and you can be drawn to them yourself. Some-

DESTROYING SPIRITUAL PROSTITUTION

times they will take you from your marriage, but you will soon discover that your union is not what you dreamed it would be.

They can be very good church members in the beginning. They might give a lot to your ministry, but then they start trying to control you with their prophecies and their constant suspicions. They will threaten to leave if they do not get their way, and dealing with them is like walking on eggshells.

These are very complicated people to deal with. Identify that spirit in your church and pull it down. The people who have these spirits are often very nice people. They are lovely people, but they do not know what spirit is behind the actions. If you are a leader in the church, you need to help them get deliverance. I pray that God will open your eyes to deliver them, in Jesus' name. Amen!

POLITICAL PROSTITUTION

Then there is what some call a Jezebel Spirit. It is my observation that those who have this spirit always like to link themselves with those in authority, like Pharaoh and his magicians, Balak and Balaam, Ahab and his prophets, Barjesus with the deputy of Paphos:

> *And when they had gone through the isle unto Paphos, they found a certain sorcerer, a false prophet, a Jew, whose name was Barjesus: which was with the deputy of the country, Sergius Paulus, a prudent man; who called for Barnabas and Saul, and desired to hear the word of God. But Elymas the sorcerer (for so is his name by interpre-*

tation) withstood them, seeking to turn away the deputy from the faith. Acts 13:6-8

Political leaders are often prone to this spirit. They either marry a person possessing it, or they have it themselves. I was in touch with a political leader who became prominent in my country of origin. He gave his life to the Lord and went to Bible School. He would attend church and pay tithes and give offerings, but he was a spiritual prostitute. He would serve at the Lord's Table, and then he wold serve at the table of his ancestors, doing all sorts of occultic practices. He would invite you to his house or office to pray, but he would also invite sorcerers. The day I first noticed what was going on, I separated myself from him, because I could not be a party to such practices. You need to do the same.

DESTROYING SPIRITUAL PROSTITUTION PRAYER POINTS

◊ Repent for your spiritual adultery with other religions.

◊ Repent for all the false accusations and hurts you have created in churches you have attended.

◊ Repent for all the hurts you have created in past marriages.

◊ If you can possibly reach them, go and reconcile with the people you have hurt in the past.

◊ If you can, restore past relationships.

◊ Destroy every evil program for spiritual prostitution in the negative supernatural against you.

◊ Divorce the spirit of spiritual prostitution.

◊ Pray for spiritual and physical restoration, in Jesus' name. Amen!

CHAPTER 7

DESTROYING TERRITORIAL AND CULTURAL STRONGHOLDS

Then said he, Knowest thou wherefore I come unto thee? and now will I return to fight with the prince of Persia: and when I am gone forth, lo, the prince of Grecia shall come.   Daniel 10:20

Governments and political regimes and systems are often infiltrated and many times governed by demonic princes. According to this scripture verse, demonic strongholds controlled the kingdoms of Persia and Greece. Human governments and the systems by which they operate have often been demonic, from the rule of Nimrod and the Pharaohs to the oppressive Persian kings. From the Roman Caesars to Hitler, Stalin and Carl Max, all had an oppressive and demonic regime.

Some human governments are controlled by the occult, while others are controlled by Freemasonry and/or other secret orders or secret societies. In some West African settings, the people are governed by fraternities such as

Ogboni, [7] Osugbo, [8]Okonko, [9] and other occult groups like the Poro, [10] Wende [11] and witchcraft. These become strongholds in those areas. To get into these political spheres is a struggle because those seats have been dedicated to the demonic stronghold in that region, and sacrifices are renewed yearly to dedicate those seats to those particular demonic powers. The spirit of Jezebel commits fornication with those in authority in those governments, polluting them and controlling them:

> *Wherein in time past ye walked according to the course of this world, according to the prince of the power of the air, the spirit that now worketh in the children of disobedience: among whom also we all had our conversation in times past in the lusts of our flesh, fulfilling the desires of the flesh and of the mind; and were by nature the children of wrath, even as others.* Ephesians 2:2-3

The jurisdiction of demonic princes initiates vices and sinful patterns, which work in disobedience to the Gospel of Jesus Christ. Sometimes a new principality takes over and changes the times, but in many areas it is still the same age-

---

7. Also known as Osugbo in Ijèbú, it is a fraternal institution indigenous to the Yoruba language-speaking polities of Nigeria, the Republic of Bénin and Togo (https://en.wikipedia.org/wiki/Ogboni Osugbo).
8. Ibid.
9. A group similar to Ogboni, but in Igbo-speaking areas (https://en.wikipedia.org/wiki/Ogboni Osugbo).
10. The Poro, or Purrah or Purroh, is a men's secret society in Sierra Leone, Liberia, Guinea and the Ivory Coast (https://en.wikipedia.org/wiki/Poro).
11. **Define it or delete it?**

abiding situation. They proceed to program lifestyles and mindsets contrary to the course of Christ in their domain.

Other political strongholds actually persecute the Kingdom of God, like Communism, ISIS and other such demonic regimes. To enter into those strongholds to win them for Christ, you first must do spiritual warfare against the forces of darkness that control them, so that their captives can be freed from their grip. These strongholds must be dethroned and their hold broken from the spirits and minds of their victims.

CULTURAL STRONGHOLDS

There are patterns that are generally known only among people groups belonging to a certain nationality or culture because that people group is under a particular demonic principality (see Ephesians 2:2-3). For example, there is a strong ancestral and familiar spirit (and the spirit of witchcraft and the occult) over the continent of Africa, and this has become a stronghold over the African people.

As another example, in some places in Africa, the practice of female genital mutilation is carried out, and this has a strong demonic origin. A blood covenant has been honored from generations past to circumcise young girls and dedicate them to demonic strongholds in the rivers. This then becomes a part of the culture, making it a stronghold in that culture. Doing evangelism in such cultures cannot be successful without first pulling down those strongholds.

If these strongholds are not pulled down, you might see converts in your own church still bound by that culture, and the young girls in your church will be partaking of the Table of the Lord and still partaking of the table of cults that covenant them to demons.

The spirit of witchcraft is a stronghold in the United Kingdom. Demonic forces have been imported from ancient Egypt, Rome, Babylon, India and Africa into the culture. Fraternities and various orders have also developed throughout the history of this nation. With the opening up of the European Union, London and other major cities in the UK have received Eastern European demonic practices and a strong influence of gypsy spirits that are building strongholds within these cities.

North America has embraced most of the Western European gods, making it a stronghold of witchcraft and rebellion. Rebellion is the strongman, and it has opened doors to secularism, individualism and humanism. The stronghold over Native Americans is witchcraft, and with the spirit of witchcraft comes the spirit of poverty that exists among many Native Americans.

South America has a strong influence of native Indian culture, backed with African and European demonic strongholds that have been built up there from the time of slavery when they were colonies of the European powers. The Caribbean is a melting pot of African and Asian demonic strongholds. Witchcraft, Voodoo, Spiritism and Black Magic are the strongmen there. The cultures and religions from the Caribbean to South America are all influenced with syncretism [12] into Catholicism.

---

12. Religious syncretism exhibits the blending of two or more religious belief systems into a new system, or the incorporation into a religious tradition of beliefs from unrelated traditions (https://en.wikipedia.org/wiki/Syncretism).

DESTROYING TERRITORIAL AND CULTURAL STRONGHOLDS

See, I have this day set thee over the nations and over the kingdoms, to root out, and to pull down, and to destroy, and to throw down, to build, and to plant.
Jeremiah 1:10

- ◊ Identify the strongman over your national borders (see Acts 19:28 and 34).

- ◊ Identify the strongman over your ethnic origin or origins (for both your mother and father's side).

- ◊ Pray and confess the sins of those in authority and every ancestral sin that has brought the curse (see Nehemiah 1:6).

- ◊ Break every political covenant and altar with territorial spirits (see Jeremiah 1:10).

- ◊ Break every ancestral covenant and altar belonging to your ethnic origin or origins.

- ◊ Nail those curses to the cross of Jesus Christ, the Son of God (see Colossians 2:14-15).

- ◊ Take authority against every demonic spirit that might want to enforce those covenants. Trample on them, bind them and drive them out, in the name of Jesus Christ, our Lord (see Luke 10:19).

- ◊ Come against anyone in politics or along that generational line that would want to renew covenants with them, in Jesus' name (see Deuteronomy 25:19).

- ◊ Loose everyone bound by that covenant, in Jesus' name (see Matthew 16:19).

Chapter 8

DESTROYING MENTAL STRONGHOLDS

For though we walk in the flesh, we do not war after the flesh: (for the weapons of our warfare are not carnal, but mighty through God to the pulling down of strong holds;) casting down imaginations, and every high thing that exalteth itself against the knowledge of God, and bringing into captivity every thought to the obedience of Christ; and having in a readiness to revenge all disobedience, when your obedience is fulfilled.   2 Corinthians 10:3-6

Some people are battling with strongholds in the mind. Their mind has become the battleground for demonic attacks on their lives. Mental strongholds can lead to mental breakdowns, with a spirit of mental breakdown as the strongman and the mind of the person becoming a stronghold of the demon.

THE THINKING OF THE PERSON

For as he thinketh in his heart, so is he: Eat and drink, saith he to thee; but his heart is not with thee.   Proverbs 23:7

If someone does not think they need deliverance or does not believe that there are demonic forces after them (even though there are), it is difficult to deliver them. The devil has built a stronghold of lies in their minds. If a person has a religious belief that contradicts what you want to do for them, those religious spirits will create a doubt in their minds. Satan's greatest deception is letting people believe that he does not exist and getting them to believe that God is the doer of whatever happens to them — good or bad.

TRAGIC EVENTS

Traumatic events such as divorce, the death of a loved one, rejection from parents or family members, rape, incest, family conflicts, shame in the family, miscarriages and bitterness can all build strongholds in the minds of those who are affected by them. These strongmen can even be the cause of these tragedies, to create a pathway to build strongholds in the lives of these people.

Job thought that God was the one afflicting him:

Though he slay me, yet will I trust in him: but I will maintain mine own ways before him.   Job 13:15

Job knew nothing about the devil, so he was blaming God for his troubles. Unfortunately that is the plight of many believers and non-believers alike out there in the world today. "God is responsible for my problems. He is to blame," they think and say.

Tragic events can open doors for people to hate others and develop bitterness toward God, the Church, family and/or other people. Racist spirits also manifest themselves in such instances. When doors are opened to these spirits, their victims are turned into another person. Their mindset changes, and controlling spirits take over their emotions.

Some people who had been sexually molested as a child are left with emotional damage. Tragic events like these can open doors to demons for sexual perversion, stubbornness and rebellion against parents. Too often, tragic events open doors to demonic infestations of various kinds.

TORMENTORS

And his fellowservant fell down at his feet, and besought him, saying, Have patience with me, and I will pay thee all. And he would not: but went and cast him into prison, till he should pay the debt. So when his fellowservants saw what was done, they were very sorry, and came and told unto their lord all that was done. Then his lord, after that he had called him, said unto him, O thou wicked servant, I forgave thee all that debt, because thou desiredst me: shouldest not thou also have had compassion on thy fellowservant, even as I had pity on thee? And his lord was wroth, and delivered him to the tormentors, till he should pay all that was due unto him. So likewise shall my heavenly Father do also unto you, if ye from your hearts forgive not every one his brother their trespasses. Matthew 18:29-35

Jesus taught us in this passage to forgive all who trespass against us. We must not hold grudges against those who offend us, and we must make a conscious effort to forgive those who have transgressed against us. Jesus even admonished us to forgive, pray for and do good things for those who spitefully use us and persecute us. This is how we show ourselves true children of our heavenly Father:

> *But I say unto you, Love your enemies, bless them that curse you, do good to them that hate you, and pray for them which despitefully use you, and persecute you; that ye may be the children of your Father which is in heaven: for he maketh his sun to rise on the evil and on the good, and sendeth rain on the just and on the unjust.*
>
> Matthew 5:44-45

In the account in Matthew 18, the lord forgave the man his grave debts, but then he refused to forgive his fellow servant his small debt. The result was that the lord heard about what he had done and put him in prison, delivering him to *the tormentors* (torturers), until he could pay his debt.

I know a lady who was hurt by her husband. He left her for another woman, and she was left to care for their children. She was very bitter about this, and she hated him so intensely that she tried all that she could to retaliate and to turn the hearts of the children against him and cause them to hate him too. She was so full of hatred that she began to get ill. She developed arthritis.

Hatred, bitterness and unforgiveness can open doors to spirits of infirmity (tormentors) that can torture you for the bitterness you hold inside. Are you full of hate? Do you spend your time devising evil plans against those who have offended you? Whenever you come across someone who has offended you, does that cause you to get agitated and want to burst out in anger? If so, this is not good for your health. Demons can be the cause of this or can capitalize on it and inflict you with infirmities like arthritis, high blood pressure or stroke.

Worries and anxieties can also result in a mental breakdown. They can bring oppression to your mind, weighing it down because of the responsibilities laid upon it:

> *Therefore I say unto you, Take no thought for your life, what ye shall eat, or what ye shall drink; nor yet for your body, what ye shall put on. Is not the life more than meat, and the body than raiment? Behold the fowls of the air: for they sow not, neither do they reap, nor gather into barns; yet your heavenly Father feedeth them. Are ye not much better than they?*   Matthew 6:25-26

Many times murderers and rapists are tormented because of the blood of the innocent they have slain. They begin to see in their minds the personages they have killed or raped, until they suffer a mental breakdown.

During the rebel war in Sierra Leone that lasted for about eleven years, many innocent people were killed. Pregnant women and young girls were raped. Infants and aged alike had their limbs chopped off. After the war we encountered a number of the rebels living in the streets with mental breakdowns. The hideous atrocities they had committed left them in demonic torment. Others were given to drugs, and that did further damage to their brains.

Drugs can also open the door to spirits of addiction and mental breakdown. Tormenting spirits then begin to torture the mind of the person, they begin to hallucinate, and their body fluids flowed out of them, and they begin to be emotionally imbalanced.

People who have given themselves to nudity and/or pornography or any kind of sexual fantasy can build images of lusts in their minds that can then become a stronghold against them. These images can become demonically controlling, so much so that it does not matter how hard they try to not think about it, the images come at will. This can become a demonic obsession, and the spirits responsible for it are called unclean spirits. They defile the minds of their captors.

Some Christians cannot control such thoughts. Even when they are praying, they see nudity and lust. Such people must first repent for viewing pornography and for going to strip clubs and other places where there is nudity, and they must repent of the evil thoughts they have entertained. Then they need to take authority over these spirits and refuse to feed that addiction ever again, if they are to be permanently delivered.

I prayed for a young lawyer to be delivered from this spirit of lust. He would be driving along in his car and when he passed a woman, he would find a place to park the car, and he would follow the woman, imagining himself having sex with her. He recognized that he was becoming a stalker, so he came to us for help, and he got his deliverance. Praise God! Jesus is still the Deliverer!

DESTROYING MENTAL STRONGHOLDS

A mental breakdown can also come as a curse. God told the people of Israel that they would be cursed with madness, blindness and heart attacks if they turned from following Him:

> *The LORD shall smite thee with madness, and blindness, and astonishment of heart.*
> Deuteronomy 28:28

LYING SPIRITS

All lies originate with Satan, for he is the father of them:

> *Ye are of your father the devil, and the lusts of your father ye will do. He was a murderer from the beginning, and abode not in the truth, because there is no truth in him. When he speaketh a lie, he speaketh of his own: for he is a liar, and the father of it.*
> John 8:44

There are people who are so natural at telling lies that the truth they think they know is nothing but a lie. They even lie when there is no cause for it. They are controlled by a spirit of lies, so they simply cannot stop lying. Truth has become alien to them, and it is hard for them to believe what others say. Because they lie, they think that others are like them.

All forms of lying is evil. White or black lies and exaggerations are all lies and all evil. Lying is a part of the old nature:

> *Lie not one to another, seeing that ye have put off the old man with his deeds; and have put on the new man, which is renewed in knowledge after the image of him that created him.*
> Colossians 3:9-10

Lying is also dangerous because it becomes hard to believe someone who has been caught telling lies.

Demons lie. That is their nature. A group of believers was delivering a girl from a lying spirit, and she said to them, "One of you has just committed fornication, and you want to come and drive me out?" The brethren, each suddenly suspicious of the other, decided to leave her alone and go home. But she was lying. The result, however, was that the mission of the demon was accomplished. His victim was left undelivered.

People who have been involved in lodges and other fraternities, cults and witchcraft have been lied to. Those who orient them lie about who Jesus really is, and they lie about the powers they possess. It is only when these people encounter true Christians that they begin to understand the limitations of their powers:

> *And he said, I will go out, and be a lying spirit in the mouth of all his prophets.*
> *And the Lord said, Thou shalt entice him, and thou shalt also prevail: go out, and do even so. Now therefore, behold, the Lord hath put a lying spirit in the mouth of these thy prophets, and the Lord hath spoken evil against thee.*
> 2 Chronicles 18:21-22

Lying spirits are seducing and enticing. They patronize you and tell you what you want to hear. They give you false hope and then lead you to your fall. Marriages have been destroyed by lying spirits. Wars, murders and deaths have all been the work of lying spirits:

> *Now the Spirit speaketh expressly, that in the latter times some shall depart from the faith, giving heed to seducing spirits, and doctrines of devils; speaking lies in hypocrisy; having their conscience seared with a hot iron.*
>
> 1 Timothy 4:1-2

We are living in days when the prophetic ministry has blessed so many lives and encouraged the Body of Christ, but in the midst of this, Satan's ministers have transformed themselves as ministers of God, using divination to seduce God's people and lead them astray for gain. Church splits, marriage breakups, marrying the wrong person, going into the wrong business or with the wrong business partners has all occurred because of a prophecy someone received. Today we have prophetic phone lines, much like the psychic phone lines that have been common for years. And people are paying for these prophecies. Prophets today prophesy at will. They seem to be able to hear God's voice at anytime — for an offering, that is.

SOOTHSAYING AND DIVINATION

Pastors need to be careful today of the prophets they allow in their churches. Visiting prophets should get clearance from the pastor before they should be allowed to speak to the congregation, especially prophets you do not know. Prophets can even be saying the right things but by the wrong spirit, and before you can think about it, they have made a mess of your congregation:

> *And it came to pass, as we went to prayer, a certain damsel possessed with a spirit of divination met us, which brought her masters much gain by soothsaying: the same followed Paul and us, and cried, saying, These men are the servants of the most high God, which shew unto us the way of salvation. And this did she many days. But Paul, being grieved, turned and said to the spirit, I command thee in the name of Jesus Christ to come out of her. And he came out the same hour.* Acts 16:16-18

A sorcerer in Ghana revealed that there were more than a thousand Christian prophets in that country who had come to him for powers. Many of those prophets are using the spirit of divination. One prophet was even said to a lady that he could tell her the color of panties she was wearing. Sometimes I wonder about the relevance of some of the words coming from these so-called prophets. Their word bears no edification or deliverance. It only shows a knowing and that's all.

MIND CONTROL

One lady minister invited me to preach in her church, but she had prepared the message I should preach. She was literally telling me what to preach. The question is: if she already had a sermon, why didn't she preach it herself? I sensed a spirit of control.

Some pastors, wives, husbands, children, bosses and others are good at mind games. They possess the spirit of witchcraft to manipulate and control the minds of others. For some people, it is like another person living in their mind. They live the other person's life and think their thoughts.

Every kind of mind control must be broken. We are only told to have the mind of Christ and to follow our leaders to the extent to which they themselves follow the Lord Jesus Christ. In many churches, no one is allowed to think outside the box. There is no "Come and let's reason together," no room for more knowledge or spiritual growth, because they have it all together. They have arrived, and you are deemed rebellious or a witch if you challenge any of their practices. I pray that God breaks down every mind-controlling spirit in the minds of His saints, in Jesus' name. Amen!

DESTROYING MENTAL STRONGHOLDS PRAYER POINTS

◊ Repent of anything you have done that has allowed strongholds to develop and control your mind.

◊ Bind every mind-controlling spirit and command them to loose your mind in Jesus' name. Amen! (see 2 Corinthians 10:3-5).

◊ Cast down imaginations, thoughts and mindsets that are in opposition to the mind and knowledge of Christ and bring them into the obedience of Christ Jesus (see 2 Corinthians 10:3-5).

◊ Resist any thought or imagination that tries to control your mind (see James 4:7-8).

◊ Renew your mind by reading and meditating on the Word of God every day (see Psalm 119:78).

Chapter 9

IDENTIFYING THE SPIRITUAL STRONGMAN

Or else how can one enter into a strong man's house, and spoil his goods, except he first bind the strong man? and then he will spoil his house.   Matthew 12:29

Deliverance cannot be complete without a person being delivered from the strongman that has bound him. Demonic gods manifests themselves in different cultures under different names, but the manifestations are basically the same. I want to give you a list of these demonic gods and the things they are primarily responsible for. In deliverance, you bind the strongman first and take his armor from him. Then you can clean the house of what is left:

When a strong man armed keepeth his palace, his goods are in peace: but when a stronger than he shall come upon him, and overcome him, he taketh from him all his armour wherein he trusted, and divideth his spoils.
                                    Luke 11:21-22

BREAKING DOWN STRONGHOLDS

NAMES OF DEMONIC DEITIES

What say I then? that the idol is any thing, or that which is offered in sacrifice to idols is any thing? But I say, that the things which the Gentiles sacrifice, they sacrifice to devils, and not to God: and I would not that ye should have fellowship with devils. Ye cannot drink the cup of the Lord, and the cup of devils: ye cannot be partakers of the Lord's table, and of the table of devils. 1 Corinthians 10:19-21

Zeus (Greek), Jupiter (Roman) and Amun (Egyptian) are all names of supreme deities worshipped among different people groups, but they were the same god. In each culture, they were known as the king of the gods. Then you have the queen of the gods. These include: Hera (Greek) and Juno (Roman). Apollo (Greek and Roman), Horus (Egyptian), Aine (Celtic), Kumudi (Hindu), Sophia (Gnostic) and Tefnut (Egyptian) are all sun gods, the god in charge of the solar powers.

Aphrodite (Greek), Venus and Cupid (Roman), Hathor (Egyptian), Lilith (Hebrew), Astarte (Canaanite), Oshun (Nigerian) and Radha (Hindu) are the god of sexual lusts and beauty. Their followers call them gods of love. Hades (Greek), Pluto (Roman), Nephthys (Egyptian) and Hina (Hawaiian) are all the god of the underworld or demon of death. Dionysus (Greek), Bacchus and Diana (Roman), Osiris (Egyptian), Mawu (West African), Oya (Nigerian) and Arawa (East African) are all considered to be the god of fertility, parties and celebrations. These are all lunar spirits, sky spirits and spirits in heavenly places.

IDENTIFYING THE SPIRITUAL STRONGMAN

I was once ministering deliverance to a lady who told me that she was under a lunar spirit. She said that during a full moon she would always have such a strong urge for sex that she felt like going out of the house and grabbing the first man she could find.

Mars (Roman), Neptune (Roman), and Oya (Nigerian) are the god of war. The god of the seas is Leviathan (Hebrew) and Mamie Wata (African), and the god of rivers is Buk (Sudanese) and Anaulikatsai'x (Native American). Vulcan is the god of fire. Many of the Spiritist churches, otherwise called "White Garment churches," and the Revivalist Pukumina Church of Jamaica all consult water spirits. Sorcerers who curse by lightening and thunder sacrifice to Vulcan.

The god of vengeance and destruction is Kali Ma (Hindu) and Nephthys (Egyptian). Lastly, the god of fertility (who is consulted by women who want to get pregnant) is variously called Asase Yaa (West African), Diana (Roman), Ostara (Anglo-Saxon), Morrigan (Celtic) or Demeter (Greek).

DEMONIC GROUPINGS

There are demonic groupings:

When the unclean spirit is gone out of a man, he walketh through dry places, seeking rest, and findeth none. Then he saith, I will return into my house from whence I came out; and when he is come, he findeth it empty, swept, and garnished. Then goeth he, and taketh with himself seven other spirits more wicked than himself, and they enter in and dwell there: and the last state of that man is worse than the first. Even so shall it be also unto this wicked generation.   Matthew 12:43-45

And he asked him, What is thy name?
And he answered, saying, My name is Legion: for we are many.   Mark 5:9

We see here that demons go and find other demons and bring them to their host to build strongholds in the life of that individual. I tell people that salvation from sins is a prerequisite for deliverance from demons. It is simple. If you are not saved, I don't pray for your deliverance from demons. If there is a case in which a person is not in their right mind to be able to accept Jesus as Savior and Lord, then it is understandable. But if the person is in his right mind, he must be saved first before deliverance.

If the person is not saved and is delivered, what happens when the demon comes back, and Jesus is not living in that person's life? He goes and brings other demons with him, and the last stage of the person is worse than the first. So what is the good in driving away the demon in the first place? You have now made the person's life worse than at the first. So let the person in need of deliverance be saved first.

It is fairly common that where you find one spirit, you will find others of the same grouping. In the people we have been ministering to for deliverance, we have observed the demonic groupings pattern you will see below. For you to effectively minister to any person, you need to observe these demonic patterns.

ADDICTIVE SPIRITS

Demons given to addiction, to drugs, alcohol and nicotine can open doors to other demonic personalities. These include: demons of sexual immorality, violence, anger, sleep and theft. The presence of one opens the door to other demonic entities, to help the evil one fulfill his demonic goals.

SEXUAL DEMONS

Sexually promiscuous demons, in their grouping, include homosexuality, lesbianism, bestiality, orgies, pornography, bisexuality, masturbation, sexual lusts and sexual fantasies, adultery and rape. Although they may not all appear together, on many occasions the temptation can be there.

EMOTIONAL-CONTROLLING SPIRITS

Demonic spirits that group under emotional controlling spirits are: indecision, procrastination, dual personalities, manipulation, control, negative self-image, insomnia, alienation, pride and anger.

SPIRITS OF DEATH

Demons of suicide and suicidal thoughts tend to include: uncontrollable anger, rage, murder, hatred and a heart that devises murder.

Identifying the strongman will enable you to drive him out, in Jesus' name.

BINDING THE SPIRITUAL STRONGMAN PRAYER POINTS

◊ You need to repent if you have been involved in the worship of the triangular powers, horoscope, sea and river spirits or forest spirits.

◊ You need to repent for anything you have allowed yourself to be dominated by through whatever addiction you have been empowered by.

◊ You need to renounce these earth-bound and heaven-bound spirits, including spirits from the underworld, and if you have anything that belongs to them, you need to burn it.

◊ You need to forgive and release anyone who has abused you in the past.

◊ You need to identify the strongman over your life and all the demons in its grouping, renounce him and all his cohorts, bind them and command them to go, in Jesus' name.

◊ You need to renounce the spirit of addiction and command him to go, in Jesus' name.

◊ You need to crucify and resist the negative disciplines of the flesh and the mind from its old ways of thinking and living.

Chapter 10

DESTROYING NEGATIVE ALTARS

And in process of time it came to pass, that Cain brought of the fruit of the ground an offering unto the LORD. But unto Cain and to his offering he [God] had not respect. And Cain was very wroth, and his countenance fell.
                                                    Genesis 4:3 and 5

For the life of the flesh is in the blood: and I have given it to you upon the altar to make an atonement for your souls: for it is the blood that maketh an atonement for the soul.   Leviticus 17:11

The building of altars goes all the way back to ancient times. From Cain and Abel to ancient Egyptian, Babylonian and Hittite civilizations, men raised up altars to their chosen god. Some of these were crude raised platforms made of dirt, but others were more elaborate, made of stones, carved rocks or elaborate articles of furniture. All of these altars were places of sacrifices to the gods. They were places where humans, animals, birds, fruits and vegetables were offered to deities in worship and where prayers and covenants were made.

The locations where these altars were erected were very significant in themselves. They were places where humans experienced the sighting of supernatural beings (see 2 Samuel 24:16-25), places they where they had been told in dreams or visions to go (see Genesis 22:1-14), or places where significant incidences occurred (see Genesis 28:11-22). These became places of contact with the supernatural — whether positive or negative.

The earliest record from the Scriptures where an altar was built was in the story of Cain and Abel, the sons of Adam and Eve. These sons of Adam came to their respective altars with sacrifices to offer to God. From this, we see that some deities require one type of sacrifice, and others require other kinds of sacrifices. The true God only accepted sacrifices that required the shedding of blood.

Some of you who are reading this book may not be saved. If that is so, then quite possibly you are experiencing a lot of warfare. Others who are saved may also be experiencing severe warfare. Demons seem to be coming against you, more than against other Christians, and you are wondering why. Life, for you, seems to be a constant struggle. There is a possibility that an ancestral or parental demonic altar has been consulted on your behalf, or you have consulted or erected one yourself, and that altar is speaking against you.

For example, you may have consulted an Obeah Man or juju man or gone to a Spiritualist or Baba to help you give birth to a child, and one of these goddesses has been consulted to help you bear the child. It may also be that someone has been using demonic powers against you, and a friend has taken you somewhere to help you get protection against these forces. The person you went to for help is also dealing with the dark powers. Remember that Satan cannot drive out Satan. What you have done was to consult a demonic altar, and you have become a partaker of that altar:

> *And Jesus knew their thoughts, and said unto them, Every kingdom divided against itself is brought to desolation; and every city or house divided against itself shall not stand: and if Satan cast out Satan, he is divided against himself; how shall then his kingdom stand.*
>
> Matthew 12:25-26

It may also be that someone has made incisions in your body or given you a cauldron to put under your bed or a chain to put around your neck or a bangle or some other object to keep in your house. By obeying them in this, you have become a partaker of that demonic altar and opened your life and your house to their parade:

> *But I say, that the things which the Gentiles sacrifice, they sacrifice to devils, and not to God: and I would not that ye should have fellowship with devils. Ye cannot drink the cup of the Lord, and the cup of devils: ye cannot be partakers of the Lord's table, and of the table of devils.*
>
> 1 Corinthians 10:20-21

It may be that those powers are now coming against you because of your covenant with them. You may have accepted the Lord Jesus Christ as your personal Savior, but if you have not renounced those covenants with the evil powers, they may still be tormenting you. If you died right now, would you go to Heaven? Yes, you are not a worshipper of Satan, and you have repented to God for your sins. But now you need to renounce those covenants, and if you have anything that belongs to that dark world, you need to get rid of it. You need to do spiritual warfare against those altars that are coming against you and uproot them and pull them down.

PULLING DOWN NEGATIVE ALTARS

See, I have this day set thee over the nations and over the kingdoms, to root out, and to pull down, and to destroy, and to throw down, to build, and to plant.

Jeremiah 1:10

As we noted earlier in the book, God told Jeremiah that He has set him over nations and kingdoms, to first root out, then pull down, destroy and throw down, and all of this had to be done before he could build and plant. This is the divine order of God. Some people try to build and to plant, and somewhere in the middle of their building and planting, some bugs appear and begin to eat up their plant and stop the progress of their building. That's why, as we have already noted, in our church we encourage deliverance immediately after someone gets saved. This completes the process of their salvation.

Deliverance does not save you, in the sense of the forgiving your sins and the opening the door of Heaven to you. What it does is help you take care of things that would try to hinder the building process and the planting of the new life you have just received.

Two altars cannot stand side by side, for our God is a jealous God. As seen in Chapter 4, you cannot serve two masters. You cannot be a Christian and be a part of Freemasonry, fraternities, the occult, witchcraft, Palo Mayombe, Macumba, Candomblé, Buddhism or Umbanda. You cannot go to church on Sunday and on some other day worship in these demonic houses. One altar must come down, while the other stands erect.

God told Gideon that he must tear down his father's altar dedicated to Baal worship and build an altar to God before he could go out to fight against his enemies. Many people are not winning in spiritual warfare because they still have an altar to Satan in their home, even while they are going out to fight Satan. Does that make sense? No, and it won't work. I don't care how many offerings you give the man of God and how much praying and fasting you do, it won't work.

Gideon gave an offering to God, but he still had to pull down the altar to Baal his father's had built:

And it came to pass the same night, that the LORD said unto him, Take thy father's young bullock, even the second bullock of seven years old, and throw down the altar of

Baal that thy father hath, and cut down the grove that is by it: and build an altar unto the LORD thy God upon the top of this rock, in the ordered place, and take the second bullock, and offer a burnt sacrifice with the wood of the grove which thou shalt cut down. Judges 6:25-26

ABRAHAM'S ALTAR

On a positive note, Abraham built several altars where God promised to bless him and his seed. One of those was built at Bethel, which means "house of God." Years later, Jacob, Abraham's grandson was passing by Bethel. He went to sleep there, and the God of his grandfather appeared to him. Why? Because his grandfather, who had already died and gone on, had made a covenant with God on Jacob's behalf. Jacob was dedicated to his grandfather's God even before he was born.

And he removed from thence unto a mountain on the east of Bethel, and pitched his tent, having Bethel on the west, and Hai on the east: and there he builded an altar unto the LORD, and called upon the name of the LORD.

Genesis 12:8

And he lighted upon a certain place, and tarried there all night, because the sun was set; and he took of the stones of that place, and put them for his pillows, and lay down in that place to sleep. And he dreamed, and behold a ladder set up on the earth, and the top of it reached to heaven: and behold the angels of God ascending and descending on it. And, behold, the LORD stood above it, and said, I

DESTROYING NEGATIVE ALTARS

am the LORD God of Abraham thy father, and the God of Isaac: the land whereon thou liest, to thee will I give it, and to thy seed. Genesis 28:11-13

As the positive, so is the negative.

DELIVERANCE FROM PARENTAL DEDICATIONS

I want to give you an account of a family I was ministering to for deliverance. I will not give names for confidentiality sake, but I can tell their story. This family is from Haiti. Their father belonged to a cult whose male followers don't stay with one woman. They might spend years with one woman and then leave for another one. Many of them who belong to this cult are rich and influential people.

This man left his girlfriend for the woman whose family I am now talking about. She was afraid of this former girlfriend because she was dabbling with darker powers and so, for her own protection, she went to a sorcerer called Master. Master had a good reputation in the area, but he did not believe in God, and if someone did, he suggested that they not come to him. Master offered to protect her, but she must do certain things:

1. She must bring three stones when she next came to see him, and she must lay the three stones on his altar.
2. She must bring a dog, and some of its blood would be sacrificed. He performed his ceremonies over the dog and told her she must give the daughter

she would bear the name she called the dog. He also told her she must not become too attached to the dog because it would soon die.
3. She received other items from him and took them home with her.

She later had a girl child, and soon afterward, the dog was hit by a car and died. In time, she had three children, and those children grew and became adults. Strangely, their lives began to follow a pattern around the number 3. Nothing they did to better themselves lasted for more than three years. They all married, but none of their marriages lasted more than three years. They started businesses, but none of their businesses lasted more than three years.

The other thing that seemed to come down the family line on the mother's side was infirmities and physical complications. Both the mother and her sister had suffered infirmities similar to what one of the daughters now began to experience. These were mysterious infirmities, for doctors would diagnose the problem, but on the day of the scheduled operation, when a final test was done, the infirmity would have disappeared, and another complication had emerged, taking its place. This was not all a coincidence; it was the devil's incidence.

Three stones had been placed on the devil's altar and a dog's blood had been sacrificed. A demonic covenant had been made by the parents of these three children, and they had been dedicated to Master's altar. No wonder they had so many problems!

DESTROYING NEGATIVE ALTARS

When I met the family, the children had been saved, and yet they were still experiencing all of these negative things. They'd had a family altercation and were fighting among themselves. The truth of the matter is that these children knew nothing about what their mother had done until the day I was doing their deliverance. I interviewed the mother, and all of this was reveled. They were so shocked that one of the daughters ran from the room in disbelief. The more questions we asked, the more strange revelations emerged.

Do you know what your parents did on your behalf before you were born? Some parents have so many miscarriages that they feel that they need to go to someone for help, and often they go to the wrong people. Were you perhaps a child who came through the intervention of some demonic force? Where you sickly as a child, and if so, do you know who your parents went to for help? Often the powers of darkness seem to render some help, but they take their pay. Some of you may now be paying for the help that was rendered to you. Your singleness, infirmity, immorality or wickedness may be the pay for the help rendered at another time. These powers may make you rich, but such riches come with great sorrow. Only the blessing of God comes with no sorrow attached:

The blessing of the Lord, *it maketh rich, and he addeth no sorrow with it.*   Proverbs 10:22

Many people are seeking help, but unfortunately, they seek it in the wrong places. Instead of freeing themselves from their sorrow, their actions only add to them. May they find the help they need, in Jesus' name. Amen!

We had to break that covenant for their deliverance. We led their Mum to Christ and asked her to renounce every covenant with the powers of darkness. Up to that point, she had still been visiting those occultic people. But she was reluctant to go all the way with Christ. She was a devoted Catholic, and to this day she believes that those spirits she consulted were good. I pray that God will open her eyes.

DESTROYING NEGATIVE ALTARS PRAYER POINTS

◊ First, do some research on your family history. Ask your parents, grandparents and/or older surviving relatives and family friends to help.

◊ Forgive your ancestors and ask God to forgive them for what they brought on the family.

◊ Renounce every negative family altar in your family line.

◊ Break every covenant your ancestors made for the whole family.

◊ In Jesus' name, bind the principality, power, ruler of darkness or spiritual wickedness belonging to that altar and stop all their activities to enforce that covenant.

◊ Break every negative family pattern in your family, in Jesus' name.

◊ Resist the devil, and he will flee from you.

Chapter 11

DESTROYING NEGATIVE COVENANTS AND DEDICATIONS

And when the king of Moab saw that the battle was too sore for him, he took with him seven hundred men that drew swords, to break through even unto the king of Edom: but they could not. Then he took his eldest son that should have reigned in his stead, and offered him for a burnt offering upon the wall. And there was great indignation against Israel: and they departed from him, and returned to their own land.   2 Kings 3:26-27

A FAMILY'S JOURNEY TO DELIVERANCE

I want to begin this chapter with a family's journey to deliverance. The story started in a Caribbean island where a child was dedicated to Lucifer by her parents and grandmother. She grew up in a native Indian family that, for generations, kept a cauldron buried under a large cedar-like looking tree, where human sacrifices were periodically made.

She was rejected by her mother as a child, because of a feud between her mother and father, and grew up in the house of the same grandmother where she had been born. In that house, every mirror was covered with white sheets, and no one was permitted to see his or her reflection, even in a window glass.

Her father was from a Pukumina [13] background, and as a child she was sexually molested a number of times by him. Somehow she was able to block this out of her memory, and during her deliverance ministration, it was revealed to me. Later God opened her eyes, and she began to remember this traumatic and horrible experience of her childhood.

Often the devil does things to people in their childhood to open doors in their lives, making them prone or programed to demonic encounters in their future life. Some people seem to continually plunge into some demonic trap. Everything about their life seems to make them prone to demonic attacks.

This woman met a young man whose father was a Freemason, and they fell in love and got married. The grooms ex-girlfriend and mother teamed up against her and hired a witch doctor four blocks down the road to bewitch her. She began to experience severe attacks of witchcraft. These attacks grew worse, until they were affecting her physically, mentally, emotionally and financially. She desperately needed help.

One day she shared her heart with a colleague at work, and this woman promised to help her. She proceeded to

---

[13]. A Jamaican sect whose central feature is spirit possession with rituals characterized by drumming, dancing, and spirit possession (http://www.britannica.com/topic/Pukumina).

DESTROYING NEGATIVE COVENANTS AND DEDICATIONS

introduce her to her Palo (a spiritual leader in the Santería religion), who gave her some readings to discover the cause of her problems and where they were coming from. His reading was accurate enough; he told her exactly who her attacker was. [14] Feeling the Christian God had abandoned her, she was now initiated into the Palo Mayombe religion.

She gave a lot of money to her Palo for protection, and whatever this "godfather" asked for she provided. A cauldron containing evil spirits was prepared for her. These spirits were to be fed with chickens. The spirits, she was told, drank blood, but they were for her protection. What she was not told was that the spirits were to be sent to harm her attackers. She had just wanted protection, not to attack other people. These demons need to attack someone, and if they are not sent to attack the designated people, they will begin to attack the one who keeps them. Soon the demons turned on her and her family.

Now, she was not only experiencing attacks from a witch doctor; she was also experiencing attacks from the demons given to her to protect her. When she saw that she could get no help from Palo Mayombe, she joined Santería, [15] which, she was told, was "the good side of Palo" and that it would draw her "closer to God." When her godfather saw that she had left Palo (and he was no longer receiving her money, he joined in the attack against

---

14. Please note: Just because people sometimes give an accurate reading does not mean that they are of God.
15. Santería originated in Nigeria, and slaves carried it to the Caribbean and South America. It now has many followers there, but also in the state of Florida in the USA.

her family, hoping that this would make her come back. Now she was being attacked from every side.

Santería originated in Nigeria, and slaves carried it to the Caribbean and South America. It now has many followers there, but also in the state of Florida in the United States.

In the initiation process of that religion, you symbolically die and are reborn. You are also married to the god of the religion — regardless of your sex. During the initiation process, your "godfather" who does the initiation cleanses your head with herbs and water in a specific pattern of movement, feeding demonic elements into your head.

Some people go to Santería for healing but end up joining the religion. This lady and her family had been initiated into Stage 1 of Santería, known as The Warrior. They were given a ceremonial bath, and a necklace was given to them, which was to serve as protection from the *orichás*, or saints of the religion (actually demons). This necklace was a symbol of the *orichás'* presence in their life and must not be worn during a woman's menstrual period, during sex or when one was bathing. In a nutshell, this family was now married to the demonic spirit of that religion.

At the time the woman was being initiated into Santería, she was pregnant, and she was told that the baby she was carrying would be a *babalawo*, a Yoruba word meaning "father of the secrets" or "father of the mysteries." Another bracelet was given to her to wear around her belly for the protection of the child. History was now repeating itself in this family. She had been dedicated to Lucifer as a child, and now her child was being dedicated to the devil from the womb. The family also collected another cauldron, this one from Santería.

Later, the woman left Santería and gave her life to Jesus Christ as her personal Lord and Savior, but she joined a church that knew very little about the powers of darkness. Her children began to have visitations from demonic personages and began to misbehave dramatically, even at home. The attacks against the family only intensified.

Her enemies began to consult ancestral family spirits to attack her, and the spirits of Palo and Santería became strong against them. Late one night, while seated at her computer, she felt a strong demonic presence behind her. The figure of the personage she saw was Mahomet, a black goat-like demonic creature with wings. This demon placed his hands behind the back of her head and opened a door there. She felt a cold breeze enter her head, and from that time onward, she began having attacks on her head.

She explained to her pastor all what she and her family was going through and was told that it was all in her head. This was no surprise. Many people who suffer as this woman did are told that it's all in their head.

She also told her pastor how her children were acting under these demonic powers, but instead of helping her, the pastor called Social Services and reported her. If you are a pastor and you are reading this, if you cannot help your people because you don't know much about the deliverance ministry, either send them to someone who knows about spiritual warfare or get those who understand it to come to your church and train a deliverance team for you. Every church needs a deliverance ministry, especially at this time when the powers of darkness are intensifying their activities.

The deliverance of this family took a very long time, and although the woman is free, she still has to resist further interference from these demons. They still want to come in, but she is resisting them. She is fighting the good fight of faith, laying hold of the life God has given her. Praise the Lord that this family met someone who understood their suffering, and God brought them deliverance.

DEMONIC SNARES

Unforgiveness, substance abuse (as with drugs and alcohol), obtaining demonic objects from false religions and the occult, blood covenants and incisions all open gates to the powers of darkness. Being a member of the occult or being a follower of a false religion and living an undisciplined lifestyle are all invitations to demonic interference with our lives. God said to Israel through Moses:

> *And I will set thy bounds from the Red sea even unto the sea of the Philistines, and from the desert unto the river: for I will deliver the inhabitants of the land into your hand; and thou shalt drive them out before thee. Thou shalt make no covenant with them, or with their gods. They shall not dwell in thy land, lest they make thee sin against me: for if thou serve their gods, it will surely be a snare unto thee.*
> Exodus 23:31-33

DESTROYING NEGATIVE COVENANTS AND DEDICATIONS

God has warned His children against making covenants with people of other religions or serving their gods. He said that if we do this, it will become a snare to us, just as they were to this family. In fact, God said we must destroy demon influences. They profess to help us, but they do not. They are only snares to trap you:

Take heed to thyself, lest thou make a covenant with the inhabitants of the land whither thou goest, lest it be for a snare in the midst of thee: but ye shall destroy their altars, break their images, and cut down their groves: for thou shalt worship no other god: for the LORD, whose name is Jealous, is a jealous God: lest thou make a covenant with the inhabitants of the land, and they go a whoring after their gods, and do sacrifice unto their gods, and one call thee, and thou eat of his sacrifice; and thou take of their daughters unto thy sons, and their daughters go a whoring after their gods, and make thy sons go a whoring after their gods. Thou shalt make thee no molten gods.
Exodus 34:12-17

BREAKING THE HEDGE

Satan wants to break down your hedge:

Hast not thou made an hedge about him, and about his house, and about all that he hath on every side? thou hast blessed the work of his hands, and his substance is increased in the land.
Job 1:10

BREAKING DOWN STRONGHOLDS

He that diggeth a pit shall fall into it; and whoso breaketh an hedge, a serpent shall bite him.   Ecclesiastes 10:8

God has built a hedge around us, just like He did around Job. It is for our protection. The devil professes that he can help when people are in trouble, but it is all a snare to trap you. What they tell you to do breaks the hedge you have around you, and as you lower your defenses, that old serpent will raise himself and bite you.

DESTROYING NEGATIVE COVENANTS AND DEDICATIONS PRAYER POINTS

◊ Break every parental or ancestral dedication of your life to the powers of darkness and renounce them, in Jesus' name. Amen!

◊ Repent and renounce every false religion you have been involved with.

◊ Renounce every blood covenant you have made.

◊ Destroy and dispose of every cauldron, bracelet or any other item in your possession belonging to the powers of darkness.

◊ Bind and command the strongman in all of the religions you have been involved with and bind and command all demons to leave you, in the name of Jesus Christ.

CHAPTER 12

DEFEATING THE POWERS IN THE HEAVENLIES

And God said, Let there be lights in the firmament of the heaven to divide the day from the night; and let them be for signs, and for seasons, and for days, and years: and let them be for lights in the firmament of the heaven to give light upon the earth: and it was so. And God made two great lights; the greater light to rule the day, and the lesser light to rule the night: he made the stars also. And God set them in the firmament of the heaven to give light upon the earth, and to rule over the day and over the night, and to divide the light from the darkness: and God saw that it was good.   Genesis 1:14-18

As noted earlier in the book, the triangular powers are the sun, the moon and the stars. God made them to separate the day from the night. They are also placed in the heavens for signs and seasons. They are rulers of the day and of the night. When Lucifer was thrown to the earth, he and his cohorts made the heavens their seat of authority.

BREAKING DOWN STRONGHOLDS

For we wrestle not against flesh and blood, but against principalities, against powers, against the rulers of the darkness of this world, against spiritual wickedness in high places. Ephesians 6:12

Demonic powers now rule the atmospheric heavens, and all of creation groans and travails in pain because of the manipulation of the devil against it. The devil has manipulated them and made them instruments of evil:

For the creature was made subject to vanity, not willingly, but by reason of him who hath subjected the same in hope, because the creature itself also shall be delivered from the bondage of corruption into the glorious liberty of the children of God. For we know that the whole creation groaneth and travaileth in pain together until now.
Romans 8:20-22

Demonic powers now pose as sun, moon and star gods, otherwise called solar and lunar powers. Even the psalmist recognize the evil they possess, when he said:

The sun shall not smite thee by day, nor the moon by night. The Lord shall preserve thee from all evil: he shall preserve thy soul. The Lord shall preserve thy going out and thy coming in from this time forth, and even for evermore. Psalm 121:6-8

The sun and moon are here associated with evil powers used by demonic forces to smite by day and by night, when one goes out and comes in. The lady whose story I told in the last chapter could not go out in the daytime, as she wanted. Whenever she was out during the day, it was as if the sun was fighting her. She would have terrible headaches. During the night, when the moon came up, the story was the same. She would hold her head and scream in pain.

One evening we went out for a prayer-walk. As we were outside walking, the moon came out with great strength. It became brighter. She then began to scream in pain and sought somewhere to sit. I said to her, "Tonight we are going to do warfare against this lunar spirit." We began to pray and do warfare against it. As we did, the pain began to subside, until it disappeared, and the moon went under the clouds, until we got back to the house.

Submit yourselves therefore to God. Resist the devil, and he will flee from you. James 4:7

Demons of lusts were also assigned against her by these lunar powers. This is the woman I mentioned in an earlier chapter. Her sexual urge would intensify nearly beyond her control when the moon was up. She said it would be so intense that the only thing she wanted to do was go out and grab the first man she saw and sleep with him.

Job talked about looking at the moon in its brightness and his heart being secretly enticed:

If I beheld the sun when it shined, or the moon walking in brightness; and my heart hath been secretly enticed, or

> *my mouth hath kissed my hand: this also were an iniquity to be punished by the judge: for I should have denied the God that is above.* Job 31:26-28

Some people's temperament changes when the moon is up, as emotion-controlling spirits are unleashed against them. They have mood swings, ranging from anger to depression, emotions they cannot control. It's almost as if another being comes and possesses them, and they do crazy things. The word *lunatic* literally refers to a madness caused by the moon. Lunatics are controlled by negative lunar powers.

OPPRESSION OF THE TRIANGULAR POWERS

> *So I returned, and considered all the oppressions that are done under the sun: and behold the tears of such as were oppressed, and they had no comforter; and on the side of their oppressors there was power; but they had no comforter.* Ecclesiastes 4:1

Many are being oppressed under the sun or solar powers. I have seen many mentally deranged men walking under the sun. If you look at them, they look busy and they are sweating, but they make no progress.

> *I returned, and saw under the sun, that the race is not to the swift, nor the battle to the strong, neither yet bread to the wise, nor yet riches to men of understanding, nor yet favour to men of skill; but time and chance happeneth to*

DEFEATING THE POWERS IN THE HEAVENLIES

them all. For man also knoweth not his time: as the fishes that are taken in an evil net, and as the birds that are caught in the snare; so are the sons of men snared in an evil time, when it falleth suddenly upon them.
Ecclesiastes 9:11-12

Under normal circumstances, the fastest individuals should win the race and the strongest win the fight. The wise should prosper, and men of understanding should be rich. Right? But for some, it is not so. They fall in an evil time, and wicked solar spirits take their opportunities from them. Solomon said that they are like a fish taken in an evil net. Promising men are being taken before their time. They are caught in the devil's trap and are taken suddenly:

Wherefore he saith, Awake thou that sleepest, and arise from the dead, and Christ shall give thee light. See then that ye walk circumspectly, not as fools, but as wise, redeeming the time, because the days are evil. Wherefore be ye not unwise, but understanding what the will of the Lord is.
Ephesians 5:14-17

This passage talks about evil days. The days we are living in are certainly evil, but there are seasons or special days that have been dedicated to certain spirits. The death rates during those times and the strength of sin, worldly pleasure and immorality are stronger during those times in a particular culture or environment.

For example, among South Americans and the people of the Caribbean, the months of Carnival are dedicated to wild and immoral demons, which are worshipped with lewdness, lasciviousness, nudity, sexual immorality and wild parties. It can be very difficult even for Christians to resist the temptations of those spirits during those days. For other cultures, it is Halloween. All sorts of witchcraft practices happen during that day. In fact, the highest form of witchcraft is practiced during a full moon. In England, Fridays are given to drunkenness. It is a tradition that most people go to the pub after work to drink, so the god of drunkenness is worshipped on Fridays there.

The battle is raging. Men of God die suddenly. Ministries rise and fall suddenly. Pastors are committing suicide. Others are caught and entangled in a net of strange and immoral relationships. There is a rise of so-called prophets these days, thousands of whom, as noted earlier, practice divination, soothsaying and sorcery. They go about contaminating and polluting God's people with idols and witchcraft:

> *For such are false apostles, deceitful workers, transforming themselves into the apostles of Christ. And no marvel; for Satan himself is transformed into an angel of light. Therefore it is no great thing if his ministers also be transformed as the ministers of righteousness; whose end shall be according to their works.* 2 Corinthians 11:13-15

> *For false Christs and false prophets shall rise, and shall shew signs and wonders, to seduce, if it were possible, even the elect. But take ye heed: behold, I have foretold you all things.* Mark 13:22-23

DEFEATING THE POWERS IN THE HEAVENLIES

We are living in times when so-called men of God are consulting the forces of darkness for their power. They worship Beelzebub and Baal in the high places and call on the name of idols and sorcerers.

THE ZODIAC

And then there's the Zodiac:

And lest thou lift up thine eyes unto heaven, and when thou seest the sun, and the moon, and the stars, even all the host of heaven, shouldest be driven to worship them, and serve them, which the LORD thy God hath divided unto all nations under the whole heaven.

Deuteronomy 4:19

Many Christians would be offended if we told them they are worshipping the stars, but in actual fact, it is true. If you believe in astrology, you are a worshipper of moon gods, and you are under the influence and control of lunar powers. To some people, the mediums seen on television are their prophets. They phone in to consult concerning their dead ones, their future, their partners and their jobs. For others, it is the astrology bibles (an astrological section of newspapers and magazines). They name themselves by the names of their gods (Gemini, Scorpio, etc.) and live their lives by the daily, weekly or monthly readings of their stars (gods). These are moon worshippers.

You cannot be a Christian and, at the same time, worship the stars. If you are doing this, you need to repent of your idolatry, renounce your lunar gods and worship Jehovah and Him alone. He is a jealous God, and you cannot have another god before Him or beside Him. In fact, there is no other gods. He is God alone.

> *Thus saith the Lord the King of Israel, and his redeemer the Lord of hosts; I am the first, and I am the last; and beside me there is no God.* Isaiah 44:6

UNDER THE RULE OF THE SUN OF RIGHTEOUSNESS

When we are saved, the Scriptures say that we are placed far above principalities and powers:

> *For the Lord God is a sun and shield: the Lord will give grace and glory: no good thing will he withhold from them that walk uprightly. O Lord of hosts, blessed is the man that trusteth in thee.* Psalm 84:11-12

Because we are in Christ, our position has changed. Our operation is from a higher plane — higher than the sun, the moon and the stars and the second heavens, where the devil and his principalities dwell. When I discovered this truth, I decided to break loose from the rulings and dominion of the triangular powers. I am far above them.

It is no wonder that in the New Jerusalem there will be no need for the sun, the moon or the stars, because the Lord Himself will be our Sun:

> *And the city had no need of the sun, neither of the moon, to shine in it: for the glory of God did lighten it, and the*

Lamb is the light thereof. And the nations of them which are saved shall walk in the light of it: and the kings of the earth do bring their glory and honour into it.
Revelation 21:23-24

So I placed and positioned myself under the Lord, who is my Sun. He is the Creator of the sun, and He is the Higher Sun. He protects me from the negative operations of the triangular powers, as I go out and come in:

The L<small>ORD</small> shall preserve thee from all evil: he shall preserve thy soul. The L<small>ORD</small> shall preserve thy going out and thy coming in from this time forth, and even for evermore.
Psalm 121:7-8

Now I speak to the sun, moon and stars in this galaxy to praise and obey their Creator. And, as far as my life is concerned, I will exercise my dominion:

Praise ye him, sun and moon: praise him, all ye stars of light. Praise him, ye heavens of heavens, and ye waters that be above the heavens. Let them praise the name of the L<small>ORD</small>: for he commanded, and they were created. He hath also stablished them for ever and ever: he hath made a decree which shall not pass. Psalm 148:3-6

Spiritually speaking, the sun is no more my light by day nor the moon my light by night. Many people are living in darkness. There is no light in their lives because the sun, moon and stars that were supposed to be light have been occupied by darkness.

> *The sun shall be no more thy light by day; neither for brightness shall the moon give light unto thee: but the LORD shall be unto thee an everlasting light, and thy God thy glory. Thy sun shall no more go down; neither shall thy moon withdraw itself: for the LORD shall be thine everlasting light, and the days of thy mourning shall be ended. Thy people also shall be all righteous: they shall inherit the land for ever, the branch of my planting, the work of my hands, that I may be glorified. A little one shall become a thousand, and a small one a strong nation: I the LORD will hasten it in his time.* Isaiah 60:19-22

Our spiritual lives are no more directed by the dictates of these powers. Many Christians don't know why their spiritual lives experience ups and downs. They don't understand the cause of it. Their sun goes down and comes up, and their moon withdraws itself. Bind the triangular powers, rage a war against them, and resist them. They will flee from you.

Praise the Lord! We are the *"branch"* of His planting. Our branch has been plucked out of our old, wild, sinful and demonic vine, where the triangular powers rule, and we have been grafted into the True Vine (Jesus Christ, the Son of God). This is the work of God's hand, and that's why we can all be righteous and be made a strong nation.

OUR LORD JESUS CHRIST IS CALLED "THE SUN OF RIGHTEOUSNESS"

> *But unto you that fear my name shall the Sun of righteousness arise with healing in his wings; and ye shall go forth, and grow up as calves of the stall. And ye shall tread down the wicked; for they shall be ashes under the soles of your feet in the day that I shall do this, saith the Lord of hosts.* Malachi 4:2-3

Thank God, we are under another Sun! He is the Sun of Righteousness. That's why we can tread on the enemies named sin, sicknesses and disease, and demonic powers. And we can live right, because the Sun that rules our lives is called The Sun of Righteousness.

Therefore, no demonic power can force or compel you to sin or to live in sin. No demonic lunar or solar power can inflict you with seasonal infirmities. No emotion-controlling spirit or spirit of mental breakdown can control your mind, because of the Sun of Righteousness. He crucified sin in His flesh, hence destroying the body of sin, and by His stripes you are healed. He became a curse for you, to free you from every demonic curse. Now secure yourself under the Sun of Righteousness, just as the woman with the issue of blood did. She touched Him, and she was healed. Be healed!

DEFEATING THE POWERS IN THE HEAVENLIES PRAYER POINTS

◊ Repent of all worship of triangular powers and renounce them, in Jesus' name (see Acts 7:29-31).

◊ Destroy and get rid of objects, Zodiac signs, books, jewelry, pictures or anything in your possession that belongs to the triangular powers (see Acts 19:19).

◊ Cut yourself loose from every evil tree under the rule and reign of the triangular powers by the sacrificial blood of Jesus and affirm your spiritual attachment to the True Vine, Jesus Christ (see Matthew 16:19).

◊ Declare to the principalities and powers that your spiritual position is changed and you are no more under the negativities of the triangular powers, but are under the Sun of Righteousness (see Ephesians 1:19-23).

◊ Destroy every evil program of the devil to control your times and seasons and release your body, mind and emotions from every evil program of these powers (see Colossians 2:14-15).

◊ Take authority against every triangular spirit, bind them, destroy all their weapons and shield yourself from them with faith (see Luke 10:19).

◊ Resist the enemy's temptations, thoughts and suggestions anytime he tries to come back. Do this, and he will flee from you (see James 4:7).

CHAPTER 13

DEFEATING WATER SPIRITS

In that day the LORD with his sore and great and strong sword shall punish leviathan the piercing serpent, even leviathan that crooked serpent; and he shall slay the dragon that is in the sea.   Isaiah 27:1

Water spirits are demonic spirits living in a world under the rivers and oceans. This demonic world is controlled by the triangular powers, just as the moon controls the tides. The Jewish people called the prince of water spirits Leviathan; Africans call it Mamie Wata.

I grew up remembering two large photo frames in my grandfather's house where three generations had lived and a fourth was then living. The first portrait showed two children playing near a cliff, with an angel behind them, protecting them. The other was Mamie Wata. She was portrayed as a black woman with long, bushy black hair, and she was holding two large snakes. It was a common wall handing in homes around West Africa.

Thinking about it now, I can't imagine that I lived with Mamie Wata all of my childhood days, watching me as I slept and awoke every day. In fact, I lived with all kinds of spirits in that house. Our home was a demonic altar to ancestral spirits. Food and drink was placed on the table for the dead. In the morning, the first person who got up and remembered the food could eat it, but these were food offerings to demons.

Commonly an elderly person poured a drink libation at the doorstep and consulted ancestral familiar spirits on behalf of the household. Holes were dug in the compound, and chicken sacrifices were made. I left that house and moved to the United Kingdom, but that house didn't leave me.

In my early years in the United Kingdom, I would dream of finding myself in that house. I had to do a lot of spiritual warfare to be released from that torment. Our Lord Jesus Christ released me from that house through his death, burial and resurrection, but that did not prevent those demons from fighting to maintain control over me through all the sacrifices both I and my ancestors had made. If I had not been exposed to the truths of spiritual warfare, they would have continued to put stumbling blocks in my way and continued to fight me until they destroyed my spiritual life and laid claim to my soul. Praise the Lord that I was not ignorant of the devil's devices.

I can't remember the last time I dreamed about that house. In fact, the house was destroyed, and my aunt has built a church over that spot. When the house was demolished to make way for the building of the church, I went to the compound, laid my hands on that land and destroyed the works of the devil there, dedicating it to the Lord. Praise God for deliverance. Amen!

PUKUMINA AND OTHER CELESTIAL CHURCHES

The Pukumina revivalist churches from Jamaica and other celestial churches — Olumba Olumba Oboe, Church of the Brotherhood and Star and Ade Jobie (as they are called in Sierra Leone) are all Spiritualist churches that require their members to wash in spirits from the sea. In Sierra Leone, many of those members worship Mamie Wata and use spirits of divination. They also consult earthbound spirits, spirits of the dead and celestial spirits. They consecrate water for everything — for prayers, for bathing, for drinking, for cooking, etc. They sprinkle what they call "holy water" during their worship, and, according to them, it brings some sort of inspiration and also drives out evil spirits. They see a lot of visions in those churches and give prophecies that are intended to rule the lives of their follower.

In many of these churches, immorality is the order of the day. Still, they can pray for anything — no questions asked. They can pray for you to have another woman's husband or to get wealth by whatever means necessary. It does not matter if you are not married; if you need a child by your boyfriend, you can get their prayers. Lots of incense is also used in their services, and their prophets carry some sort of wand.

The people who attend these churches worship barefooted, and some of them never wear shoes, wherever they go. Their prayers are done mostly with the lighting of candles, and they offer sacrifices of animal blood. Late at night, they go to the beaches to worship and consult the water spirits. The rhythm of their drum beating can become controlling, and many who have left these churches testify that when they pass by, if the drums are being beaten, they can hardly control their bodies from being overpowered by the sound of those drums.

On several occasion, in Sierra Leone (my land of origin), some of the prophets from these groups have gone to the ocean to consult their marine spirits and, after making sacrifices to them, a wave came and swept them away. Some were never found.

I had a neighbor who was sharing a house with one of these prophets, and he told me that nearly every night he overheard the man in his room fighting with Mamie Wata. Another prophet had a serpent who would swim on the "holy water" which he then gave to his people to consecrate them.

Clearly these churches are not of God. These people are Spiritualists, not Christians. If you have been a part of any such group or have gone to them for prayers, you have been contaminated by water spirits. If you offered some sacrifice they asked you to make or partook of any of their feasts, like "Tabora," you have eaten foods offered to demons, and you will need deliverance from them.

What is your dream life like? Do your dreams always connect you to a certain river or to the sea? Do you dream that you are crossing a river in a canoe or swimming in the river or attending meetings under the sea? If so, you must have some connection with Mamie Wata. If you don't know what to do, you need to consult a genuine deliverance minister to help you through your deliverance.

During deliverance from Mamie Wata, people who have been held under her grip fight violently, clearing everything in their path. I once held a deliverance meeting on a college campus, and one of the female students was possessed by a water spirit. She told me that she had a "spirit husband" who gave her money. She had first encountered this demon one morning when she went to the stream. During her deliverance ministration, she began to swim on the tile floor, like she was swimming in a river. She swam from one end of that hall to the other, on that floor, and she did it in a flash. She was about to swim out into the street when I shouted to the others to catch her.

These are not made-up stories. They are things that I have witnessed with my own eyes. Water spirits are real. They are very immoral spirits, and they contaminate the people who submit to them and offer them as captives to the underworld. But deliverance is available to all, regardless of how far anyone they have gone into the realms of the underworld. Jesus came to set the captives free, and whom the Lord shall make free shall be free indeed:

Jesus answered them, Verily, verily, I say unto you, Whosoever committeth sin is the servant of sin. And the servant abideth not in the house for ever: but the Son abideth ever. If the Son therefore makes you free, ye shall be free indeed. John 8:34-36

DEFEATING WATER SPIRITS PRAYER POINTS

◊ Repent (turn away) from the practice of Spiritualism and ask that the blood of Jesus Christ, God's Son, cleanse you from all sins.

◊ Renounce all marine and serpentine spirits and spirits of divination, in Jesus' name.

◊ Ask that the blood of Jesus Christ, God's Son, cleanse you and your family from all contamination and pollution from marine, serpentine and divination spirits.

◊ Bind these spirits and loose yourself from their domination and control.

◊ Continue to resist them anytime they try to make contact again.

◊ Never again be entangled by Spirituality. Don't go to their places of worship, and don't eat at their feasts.

CHAPTER 14

DESTROYING HAUNTINGS

Be sober, be vigilant; because your adversary the devil, as a roaring lion, walketh about, seeking whom he may devour.   1 Peter 5:8

DEDICATED DEMONIC PLACES

There are evil spirits that make their abode in certain places of the earth. In fact, Satan is said to walk about in the earth seeking whom he may devour. Demonic forces dwell in mountains, in valleys, in forests, in temples, in churches, in occultist temples and shrines and even in some people's homes. So be careful about the places you visit.

Avoid places like cult and occultic shrines, Spiritualist churches, Free Masonry lodges, mountains that are dedicated to the worship of demons, worship places of false religions and/or for the worship of idols. These are all places dedicated and consecrated to demonic forces. Avoid demonic forests, houses used for divination, soothsaying, necromancy and crystal ball readings, brothels and cemeteries where witchcraft is practiced.

Freemasons have been known to practice consulting the dead and performing all kinds of ancestral worship. Their houses are all places of demonic residence.

The homes of the people who practice such things and the homes of people with cauldrons are all demonic addresses. Idolatrous people and people who practice ancestral worship always have a shrine to their gods in their homes. Religions like Palo Mayombe have cauldrons with demons in them, to whom they offer the blood of chickens. They host their demons in a dedicated room in their house. Some people even keep a room like this under lock and key.

HAUNTED HOUSES

If you are a homeowner, be careful whom you rent your home to. Some people can leave demons in your house and cause it to be haunted, especially if they die there without first being able to hand over their demons to someone else.

Houses become haunted for various reasons. If a house was used as a slaughter house or the offering of human sacrifices to demons, it can be left haunted with familiar spirits and the blood-sucking spirits to whom the blood sacrifice was made. If the house is used in consultation with demonic spirits and the one who consults them disobeys their laws and is killed by them, the house becomes haunted. If a demon is an ancestral spirit normally handed down from parent to child, for instance, and a parent could not hand off the demon to a child for what-

DESTROYING HAUNTINGS

ever reason before they died, the house could be haunted. Demonic spirits then roam the corridors of the house or reside in a particular room in the house. The place may contain a peculiar smell, and anytime you enter that room or the house, the hairs on your body and head will stand up. Suddenly, you begin to shiver, and cold chills run up and down your spine.

Some people actually see personages, or such personages appear to them in a dream. They see shadows passing by, and noises and voices are heard. Objects move when no one else is in the house. With some haunted houses, the owners or the people living there begin to have suicidal or murderous thoughts or are incited to commit sadistic sexual practices, depending on what kind of spirit is in the house. I have prayed over many haunted houses and driven out the spirits from them.

If the place where the house is built was once a shrine to the powers of darkness or a land belonging, for example, to native American Indians or perhaps was used as a burial ground, any house built on that site could be haunted. These people have a covenant connection with their land, making it a host to the demonic spirits they worship.

To deliver those lands and homes, you need to know their history so you can understand the demonic spirits that are or have been worshipped there. If those lands were violently taken from their rightful owners, repentance must be made and sins must be confessed. Then those demonic spirits can be challenged and commanded to leave.

WHEN BUILDING A NEW HOUSE

When you are building a new house, first do some investigation about the place and do deliverance over its soil. Address the principalities and powers in that place, and cut your land free from their dominion. Take some of the soil of that land and dedicate the very foundations of your new home to the Lord. Then, after the house is built, dedicate it to the Lord.

If you are moving to a new home or property, investigate the area and the former occupants and the reason they moved. You may find something interesting. Only then make your decision about whether or not this is where you should live. If it is a place you want to stay, you need to pray over the house, deliver it from the powers of darkness and dedicate it to the Lord. When I move to any new place, I always do this, and in the process cut that house loose from the rule and dominion of any wicked spirits in the area.

DESTROYING HAUNTINGS PRAYER POINTS

◊ Pray a prayer of repentance for visiting places you never should have visited in the first place.

◊ Renounce whatever god is worshipped there and any of their evil practices you have been involved in just by visiting such places (this includes necromancy, fortune telling, Palo Mayombe, Obeah Man, etc.).

◊ Ask the Lord to cleanse you by the blood of Jesus from all spiritual and physical contamination you might have gotten yourself involved with.

◊ Renounce and destroy every object that might have been given to you.

◊ Bind and command to leave whatever demons may have been assigned to you because of your visit to their territory.

◊ Come against every snare of the devil or counter-attack by resisting them, in Jesus' name. Amen!

CHAPTER 15

PRAYERS FOR DELIVERANCE

And it shall come to pass, that whosoever shall call on the name of the LORD *shall be delivered: for in mount Zion and in Jerusalem shall be deliverance, as the* LORD *hath said, and in the remnant whom the* LORD *shall call.*

Joel 2:32

There are specific kinds of prayers that are necessary for deliverance. Since some of you reading this book may be new to the Christian faith or may not understand the concept of Christian prayer and the rules governing them, I want to take the time here to name and write down some prayers that may be beneficial to you. Please say them as your own in all sincerity and truth. Say them in faith toward God and with love for God in you heart.

I understand that everyone's situation may not be the same, so please don't count the prayers sufficient for a situation which may be peculiar to you. Add and/or remove parts of the prayer which are relevant or irrelevant to you. You can even look at your own situation and then write down your own prayer or prayer points, so as not to miss any relevant area that is necessary for your deliverance.

A PRAYER OF REPENTANCE

Dear Father in Heaven,

I come to You in the name of our Lord and Savior, Jesus Christ. I have sinned against You in thought, word and deed. I was born a sinner and practiced sin. I confess all wrong doings, knowingly and unknowingly. This day I turn away from my sins, my old way of thinking and my practice of sin. I genuinely repent of my sins and I ask for your forgiveness through the death, burial and resurrection of Jesus Christ for my sins. Thank You, Father, in Heaven, for forgiving my sins, and I receive reconciliation, peace and righteousness by faith.

In Jesus' name,
Amen!

A PRAYER OF RENUNCIATION

Dear Father in Heaven,

I renounce every sin, every evil practice, covenants, initiation and dedication to the powers of darkness (<u>name them if you know them</u>), in Jesus' name I pray. All the vows I have pronounced to such powers of darkness (<u>name them</u>) I recant, in Jesus' name. I withdraw every word and renounce every practice and point of contact with those powers, in Jesus' name.

Every offering, symbolism, blood covenant, sacrifice, communion of food and drink offering, bathing, robes, other clothing, names given to me, charms and spirits assigned to me, I

PRAYERS FOR DELIVERANCE

renounce, in the name of Jesus Christ of Nazareth.

Every self-imposed curse I have pronounced on myself and my family for renouncing and revealing the secrets of this demonic group, I cancel, revoke and rescind, in Jesus Christ's name. Amen! I revoke impositions of death, accidents, infirmities, persecutions, punishments and every other evil consequence.

In Jesus Christ's name

Amen!

Please make sure that whatever you took from these demonic influences or bought in their shops (books, jewelry, charms, garments, beads, DVDs, cauldrons, etc.) is renounced and destroyed. I recommend that they be burned with fire.

A PRAYER OF CONSECRATION AND DEDICATION

Dear Father in Heaven,

I now dedicate my entire being to You, in Jesus Christ's name. I present my body as a living sacrifice, holy and accepted to You, in the name of Jesus Christ of Nazareth. My mind I consecrate to You and declare it to be the mind of Christ, in Jesus' name. I renew it with the Word of God and refute every argument, thought, imagination or high thing that would try to exalt itself above the knowledge of Christ Jesus and command them to obey the mind of Christ, in Jesus' name.

Every spirit assigned against my mind I bind, and I command them to leave in Jesus' name, and I plead the blood of Jesus over my mind, to consecrate and dedicate it to God, in Jesus' name. Cleanse my spirit, mind and body from every filthiness of the enemy, and cause a perfection of holiness in them and the fear of God in them.

In the name of Jesus Christ, our Lord,
Amen!

A PRAYER OF BINDING AND LOOSING

My Father in Heaven,

You said in Your Word that whatever we bind on earth is bound in Heaven, and whatever we lose on earth is loosed in Heaven. I bind (<u>name every spirit you are aware of that has controlled you</u>), in Jesus' name. Amen! In Jesus' name, I forbid every one of your undertakings in my life, lose myself from your grip and command you to go from my life into waste places.

In Jesus Christ's name, the Son of the living God,
Amen!

Say this prayer against every single one of the demonic forces you were involved with, one after the other. Then exhale and let them go. If you know which of them is the strongman in your life, address the strongman first and command him to go with every demon he has brought in with him. Tell them all to get out with him, in Jesus' name. Amen!

USING THE NAME OF JESUS IN PRAYER

Always command demon forces to leave in Jesus' name. That name is your most important weapon against the forces of darkness:

PRAYERS FOR DELIVERANCE

That at the name of Jesus every knee should bow, of things in heaven, and things in earth, and things under the earth; and that every tongue should confess that Jesus Christ is Lord, to the glory of God the Father.   Philippians 2:10-11

The name of Jesus is the authority that is recognized in Heaven, on earth and in the underworld. All must obey the authority this name possesses because God has highly exalted the name Jesus above every other authority. Demons will obey when you utter that name:

And being found in fashion as a man, he humbled himself, and became obedient unto death, even the death of the cross. Wherefore God also hath highly exalted him, and given him a name which is above every name.
                                                            Philippians 2:8-9

Jesus defeated Satan and all his cohorts through His death, burial and resurrection. He took every authority, rule and dominion from the enemy, and God invested authority in Jesus' name to drive out demons and to extend salvation to all:

Blotting out the handwriting of ordinances that was against us, which was contrary to us, and took it out of the way, nailing it to his cross; and having spoiled principalities and powers, he made a shew of them openly, triumphing over them in it.   Colossians 2:14-15

And these signs shall follow them that believe; In my name shall they cast out devils; they shall speak with new tongues.   Mark 16:17

USING THE BLOOD OF JESUS IN PRAYER

Redemption, deliverance, salvation and victory in spiritual warfare all come through the blood of Jesus Christ, the Son of God. Use it for your salvation and deliverance and use it as a weapon against the forces of Satan. Here is a blood of Jesus confession:

Father,

I thank You that I am forgiven by the blood of Jesus Christ, the Son of God. His blood makes peace between You and me. I am reconciled and at peace with God the Father by the blood of Jesus. I am forgiven and being forgiven and will be forgiven by the blood of Jesus. I am cleansed from all unrighteousness by the blood of Jesus Christ. I come very close to God by the blood of Jesus.

I am delivered from the powers of darkness by the blood of Jesus Christ. I am protected and I overcame the wicked one and his wickedness by the blood of Jesus Christ. The blood of Jesus Christ healed me of all infirmities, and by the blood of Jesus Christ I escape every death plan and death threat of the devil. I shall not die by any weapon of death from the enemy, in Jesus' name. I cover my life and all of mine by the saving power of Jesus Christ and release it against every power of the devil to overcome it.   In Jesus' name,

Amen!

And they overcame him by the blood of the Lamb, and by the word of their testimony; and they loved not their lives unto the death. Revelation 12:11

And the blood shall be to you for a token upon the houses where ye are: and when I see the blood, I will pass over you, and the plague shall not be upon you to destroy you, when I smite the land of Egypt. Exodus 12:13

PRAYING IN THE SPIRIT

We must pray in the Spirit:

Praying always with all prayer and supplication in the Spirit, and watching thereunto with all perseverance and supplication for all saints. Ephesians 6:18

But ye, beloved, building up yourselves on your most holy faith, praying in the Holy Ghost. Jude 1:20

We are taught to pray with all kinds of prayers in the Holy Spirit and that the Holy Spirit also makes intercession for the saints according to the will of God. Praying in the Holy Spirit also builds your faith, when you are ministering under such circumstances. It also unites you and the Holy Spirit of God, Who helps you in the ministration.

TAKING AUTHORITY IN PRAYER

In spiritual warfare, you submit to God and resist the devil. This is what makes the devil flee from you. So part of the "prayers" used in spiritual warfare are actually not prayers but, rather, using your authority against the powers of darkness. You are not praying to demons and begging them to leave, but you are using your authority against them as one superior to them and in a higher position of authority over them. You are given authority backed by law to enforce penalties on them, and they must obey you in the name of Jesus:

> *Behold, I give unto you power to tread on serpents and scorpions, and over all the power of the enemy: and nothing shall by any means hurt you.* Luke 10:19

Your authority against the forces of darkness is given to you by God, in His Word, by the power of His Spirit, His blood and His name. Jesus drove out demons by His Word. When Satan tempted Him, he used the Word of God against him. So, stand in faith and use your authority against the powers of darkness, and watch Heaven back you up:

> *Put on the whole armour of God, that ye may be able to stand against the wiles of the devil. For we wrestle not against flesh and blood, but against principalities, against powers, against the rulers of the darkness of this world, against spiritual wickedness in high places. Wherefore take unto you the whole armour of God, that ye may be able to withstand in the evil day, and having done all, to stand.*
> *Stand therefore, having your loins girt about with truth, and having on the breastplate of righteousness; and your*

feet shod with the preparation of the gospel of peace; above all, taking the shield of faith, wherewith ye shall be able to quench all the fiery darts of the wicked. And take the helmet of salvation, and the sword of the Spirit, which is the word of God: praying always with all prayer and supplication in the Spirit, and watching thereunto with all perseverance and supplication for all saints.

Ephesians 6:11-18

ACCEPTING THE LORD JESUS AS YOUR LORD AND SAVIOR

I frequently tell people that I won't pray for them for deliverance from the powers of darkness if they are not born again. If Jesus is not the Lord of their lives, they could get delivered and then go away and continue the lifestyle that brought about their evil predicament and end up being worse off than they were before:

When the unclean spirit is gone out of a man, he walketh through dry places, seeking rest, and findeth none. Then he saith, I will return into my house from whence I came out; and when he is come, he findeth it empty, swept, and garnished. Then goeth he, and taketh with himself seven other spirits more wicked than himself, and they enter in and dwell there: and the last state of that man is worse than the first. Even so shall it be also unto this wicked generation.   Matthew 12:43-45

It is only right that you accept Jesus as your Lord and Savior, to keep you continually delivered from the powers of darkness. It is not just about getting delivered from demons, but, rather, about living a victorious lifestyle by becoming a new creation in Christ Jesus. If you want to find faith in Christ Jesus, please genuinely say the following prayer:

A PRAYER OF FAITH IN JESUS CHRIST

Dear Father in Heaven,
  I am truly sorry for my sins. Today I repent of my sins. I turn away from them completely without any reservation whatsoever. With my whole heart I believe that Jesus Christ died for my sins, He was buried and resurrected to justify me from all wrong doing. With my mouth I confess that Jesus Christ is the Son of God and Lord of my life.
  Lord Jesus, I thank You for forgiving me of all my sins and making me a new creature.
In Jesus' name I pray, with thanksgiving,
Amen!

If you said this prayer in faith, you are now a child of God. You are saved and delivered from the powers of darkness. You are now translated into the Kingdom of God, and you have redemption through the blood of Jesus. You are reconciled to God through that same blood, and you are at peace with God. The old is gone, and He has made all things new. You are now a child of God and a citizen of the Kingdom of God. Amen!

CHAPTER 16

KNOWING YOUR REDEMPTION

And having spoiled principalities and powers, he made a show of them openly, triumphing over them in it.
                                              Colossians 2:15

As you have read, you may have observed that there are at least one or two areas where there might be a stronghold in your life, for instance, a situation you may have prayed and fasted about and even gone for counseling about, but to no avail. It may be a compelling habit or a prolonging situation that won't leave you. This could eventually endanger your life or ruin your credibility and everything you have built, and deliverance may be what is needed.

DELIVERANCE HAS ALREADY BEEN ACHIEVED

First you need to understand that deliverance is not something yet to be achieved. Deliverance has already been achieved on the cross of Jesus on Calvary:

Who hath delivered us from the power of darkness, and hath translated us into the kingdom of his dear Son: in whom we have redemption through his blood, even the forgiveness of sins.   Colossians 1:13-14

BECOMING MORE THAN A CONQUEROR

Paul asked several questions in the eighth chapter of Romans:

What shall we then say to these things? If God be for us, who can be against us? He that spared not his own Son, but delivered him up for us all, how shall he not with him also freely give us all things? Who shall lay any thing to the charge of God's elect? It is God that justifieth. Who is he that condemneth? It is Christ that died, yea rather, that is risen again, who is even at the right hand of God, who also maketh intercession for us. Who shall separate us from the love of Christ.   Romans 8:31-35

What shall we say to theses things?

What shall we say to all these demonic problems? The answer is simple: *"If God be for us, who can be against us?"* Who? The powers of darkness are no match for the Kingdom of Light, and no demon can match a child of God. We have authority and dominion over them, so let's use it and be free of them.

Shall He not with Him also freely give us all things?

If God did not spare His only Son, Jesus, but gave Him to be killed for us, He cannot withhold deliverance or healing from us. In fact, the delivery of His Son to death was for our healing and deliverance from the forces of darkness:

> *For the L*ORD *God is a sun and shield: the L*ORD *will give grace and glory: no good thing will he withhold from them that walk uprightly.* Psalm 84:11

Who shall lay any thing to the charge of God's elect?

"It is God that justifieth." The devil has no accusation, no covenant, no sin (ancestral, parental or individual) against you that can withstand repentance and the blood of Jesus Christ, our Lord. The only judge who has power to condemn both body and soul to Hellfire is the One who has declared you righteous and free from any wrongdoing.

Who is he that condemneth?

"It is Christ that died, yea rather, that is risen again, who is even at the right hand of God, who also maketh intercession for us." Isn't it wonderful to know that the only One who has power of condemn you is your Intercessor? He is not there to condemn you. You have passed from death to life. He is praying for you to overcome every obstacle.

Who shall separate us from the love of Christ?

Nothing can separate us from Christ's love. In Him, we have overcome everything:

For I am persuaded, that neither death, nor life, nor angels, nor principalities, nor powers, nor things present, nor things to come, nor height, nor depth, nor any other creature, shall be able to separate us from the love of God, which is in Christ Jesus our Lord. Romans 8:38-39

The devil and his cohorts cannot take you away from God's love. You are secure in His love. The devil cannot make you do anything you don't want to do. You are in charge of your life, in Jesus' name. Jesus defeated the devil. All you need to do is enforce that victory, and by enforcing the victory, you become more than a conqueror:

Nay, in all these things we are more than conquerors through him that loved us. Romans 8:37

Now that you have understanding in these facts, you need to enforce them in your daily life. You need to put Satan and his cohorts where they belong and lay hold of the salvation and victory Jesus has achieved for you on the cross of Calvary. This is what you do when you appropriate deliverance. Deliverance can be self-appropriated, or someone who understands deliverance can minister it to you.

DISCOVER TO RECOVER

The first step toward deliverance ministration is to diagnose the demonic personalities responsible for whatever is happening in your life and what caused it. This can be done through prayer and through self-diagnostics through what you have learned in this book. There is also a self-diagnostic form in my book, *Be Delivered and Stay Delivered,* which could help. The gift of discerning of spirits can come in very handy in these circumstances. God can open your eyes or the eyes of someone in the realms of the Spirit to diagnose your problem and where it is coming from.

REPENTANCE

There is no deliverance without repentance. A commandment of God must at least have been broken for the serpent to come in and bite:

> *He that diggeth a pit shall fall into it; and whoso breaketh an hedge, a serpent shall bite him. Whoso removeth stones shall be hurt therewith; and he that cleaveth wood shall be endangered thereby.* Ecclesiastes 10:8-9

Repentance erases the cause:

> *If we confess our sins, he is faithful and just to forgive us our sins, and to cleanse us from all unrighteousness.*
> 1 John 1:9

Remember that cleansing comes through confessing and forsaking sins.

THE MINISTRATION

I usually encourage people doing deliverance to observe a time of praying and fasting before going through deliverance ministry. This empowers them spiritually and mentally. Even Jesus spoke concerning this:

> *Then came the disciples to Jesus apart, and said, Why could not we cast him out? And Jesus said unto them, Because of your unbelief: for verily I say unto you, If ye have faith as a grain of mustard seed, ye shall say unto this mountain, Remove hence to yonder place; and it shall remove; and nothing shall be impossible unto you. Howbeit this kind goeth not out but by prayer and fasting.*
> Matthew 17:19-21

Deliverance ministry is taking authority over demonic spirits and commanding them to leave in the name of Jesus Christ. It is breaking demonic covenants and curses and renouncing them. In the process, spiritual weapons are used.

THE WEAPONS OF OUR WARFARE

Our spiritual weapons, the Bible promises, are fully capable of pulling down demonic strongholds. They pull down strongholds in the mind, spirit and emotions, as well as in the will and in the body. Demon strongholds have no choice but to obey your command:

> *(For the weapons of our warfare are not carnal, but mighty through God to the pulling down of strong holds;) casting down imaginations, and every high thing that exalteth itself against the knowledge of God, and bringing into captivity every thought to the obedience of Christ.* 2 Corinthians 10:4-5

THE NAME OF JESUS

The name of Jesus is the name given under Heaven by which a man can be saved. He is the One who has all authority in Heaven and on earth. He is the One who spoiled principalities and powers. He defeated Satan and his cohorts and triumphed over them. Jesus' name has been given authority by God, and demons will be subjected to us through His name:

And the seventy returned again with joy, saying, Lord, even the devils are subject unto us through thy name. And he said unto them, I beheld Satan as lightning fall from heaven. Behold, I give unto you power to tread on serpents and scorpions, and over all the power of the enemy: and nothing shall by any means hurt you. Luke 10:17-19

We have ministered to many who, when the demons begin to manifest in them, began to scream and tell us not to mention the name of Jesus. We keep on calling Jesus, and the demons have to leave.

THE BLOOD OF JESUS

The blood of Jesus or the death of Jesus on the cross did not only forgive our sins, reconcile us to God, make Israel and us one new man in Christ Jesus and defeat sin, but it also delivered us from the forces of darkness. We actually overcame the devil by the blood of Jesus Christ. Satan's head was crushed at the cross of Jesus Christ. He lost the battle that day:

> *And I will put enmity between thee and the woman, and between thy seed and her seed; it shall bruise thy head, and thou shalt bruise his heel.* Genesis 3:15

> *And they overcame him by the blood of the Lamb, and by the word of their testimony; and they loved not their lives unto the death.* Revelation 12:11

PRAISE AND WORSHIP

We must never underestimate the power of praise and worship. The Scriptures tell us that God inhabits the praises of His people. We have encountered difficult deliverance cases, but when we begin to praise the Lord, the demonic yoke was broken because the presence of the Lord had filled the room. When the Lord arises, His enemies are scattered. In one case, as we continued praising the Lord and the yoke over the person was broken, foam began coming out of their mouth, and deliverance was complete:

> *Let God arise, let his enemies be scattered: let them also that hate him flee before him. As smoke is driven away, so drive them away: as wax melteth before the fire, so let the wicked perish at the presence of God. But let the righteous be glad; let them rejoice before God: yea, let them exceedingly rejoice.* Psalm 68:1-3

THE WORD OF GOD

Jesus drove out spirits with His Word, and in deliverance we also use the Word of God against the devil. It works in overcoming temptations from the devil, and it also works in driving them out:

> *When the even was come, they brought unto him [Jesus] many that were possessed with devils: and he cast out the spirits with his word, and healed all that were sick.*
> Matthew 8:16

Use the Word of God, for it is a living Word. It is powerful and defeats the enemy. Live by it. It is an effective weapon of warfare against all the forces of darkness. Praise the Lord for His Word! Thank You, Jesus!

There is nowhere in the Scriptures that indicates that we are to apply physical violence against the demonically oppressed or the agents of darkness. Our weapons are spiritual, not physical. Use the Word of God, not physical strength or physical weapons.

MANIFESTATIONS

Demons can manifest themselves as you minister to people who have them, so we need to understand some of these manifestations. Understanding them helps us to identify which demons are in operation.

I was ministering in a church in Kent, England, and as I started laying hands on people and praying for them, I touched a man who was covered with tattoos, and the demons began manifesting in him. He jumped onto the chairs and started cursing loudly. He had a foul spirit in him. Sadly, he left the church refusing further prayer.

A demon of lust will often cause a person being delivered to want to rip off their clothes. Emotional-controlling spirits manifest themselves through a range of mood swings, often characterized by weeping. Those who have a spirit of anger clench their fists and demonstrate rage. On many occasions the spirit of pornography and masturbation is operating in those who shake their fingers and hands uncontrollably.

For a variety of reasons, some fall to the ground and even become sick. [16] The reasons range from the effects of spirit husband and wife, water spirits, witchcraft or others. When you are praying for someone, and their eyes roll up in the heads and all you can see are the whites of their eyes, you are dealing with a spirit of death.

There are lots of other manifestations. Some are similar from one demon to another, and others are totally different. Understanding each manifestation helps to diagnose the case and consequently results in an effective ministration.

---

16. Not all falling down can be attributed to demons. Some people also fall down under the anointing of the Holy Spirit, as they receive blessings from God.

CHAPTER 17

THE CONCLUSION

I hope this book has been a blessing to your life. It cannot give all the answers for every deliverance case, but it can be an eye-opener to some things that may have been a mystery to you until now. The prayer points at the end of many chapters were intended to guide you, but one situation may differ from another. You can even make your own prayer points that are more related to your specific situation.

Although the teachings you have read here will begin to point you toward deliverance from the powers of darkness, there are a lot of things I have not written about in the book. So I would advise that you prayerfully seek for deliverance through a deliverance minister, if you think you need one. That will help you get complete deliverance.

There are many books available these days on deliverance. Some of them are good, and others are not so good or even bad. Please use spiritual discernment about what you read. You do not need to agree with everything I have said here, but instead of simply dismissing a point, take it to the Lord in prayer, and the Holy Spirit will guide you.

Because I have been in the deliverance ministry now for more than twenty years and have spent much time in the study of the Scriptures, what I have shared with you here is my understanding and my experience in the ministry. I pray that these will help you. God bless you as you journey to your complete deliverance and grant you complete victory and success, in Jesus' name. Amen!

OTHER BOOKS BY DESMOND THOMAS

Desmond Thomas

Be Delivered and Stay Delivered

The Believer's Handbook to Deliverance from the Power of Darkness

A Man after God's own Heart

Moving Successfully Toward Spiritual Continuity, Establishment and Leadership

Desmond Alphonso Thomas

BE HEALED AND STAY HEALED

MINISTRY PAGE

Those wishing to correspond with the author may do so at the following addresses:

In Africa:
Pastor Desmond A. Thomas
Ministry of the Word
P.M.B. 365
Freetown, Sierra Leone
West Africa

In Europe:
Ministry of the Word
desmondthomasministries@yahoo.com
www.facebook.com/desmondthomasministries

In the U.S.:
Ministry of the Word
c/o McDougal & Associates
www.thepublishedword.com

www.ingramcontent.com/pod-product-compliance
Lightning Source LLC
LaVergne TN
LVHW041619070426
835507LV00008B/335